# I Really Gotta Horse

## The continuing adventures of racehorse ownership

Stephen A Cawley

# Cover Notes

The cover picture shows the American actor Alan Young who died at the grand old age of 96 while I was writing this book. Apparently one of his claims to fame was that as a young actor he dated Marilyn Monroe and taught her to play the bagpipes! This strikes me as a wasted opportunity, and probably explains why he ended up talking to a horse!

Mr Ed, the talking horse was the only equine influence on the author until much later in life. In the picture Alan Young poses with Mr Ed and the author with the ill-fated Herefordshire.

For my old mate LT

This man has proved himself to be a walking encyclopedia on horse racing, however I would not recommend taking one of his tips

# CONTENTS

Acknowledgements
Introductory Notes

# Acknowledgements

Thanks to Stan Hey's book for the original idea and the following sources have been used for reference purposes.

An Arm and Four Legs, Stan Hey, Yellow Jersey Press, 1998
Horses for Courses, Anne Holland, Mainstream, 2005
The Racing Tribe, Kate Fox, Metro, 2005
The Course Inspector, Alan Lee, Collins Willow, 2001
(The above book by the late Alan Lee, was particularly useful for the *Raceday* sections, where the 'Inspector' is made reference to)
The following web addresses
Britishhorseracing.com
Racing post.com
Sportinglife.com

# Introductory Notes

Basically this book is in the form of a diary, which follows the events surrounding the author's decision to enter a horse owning syndicate.
The initial chapter explains how the syndicate came about and places it in the context of the author's previous work; "*Four Hooves and a Prayer*". Subsequent chapters cover the seven months that formed the duration of the syndicate lease.
The book keeps to the same template used in the previous work to describe the various race days.

# CHAPTER1
# EARLY DAYS

**FIRST THOUGHTS**

I had got the taste for 'horse ownership' in the odyssey that was; *'Four Hooves and a prayer'*. As Anne Holland puts it in her book 'Horses for Courses', I had been 'caught by the racing bug'. In *'Four Hooves and a Prayer'* of course I had taken out the smallest possible ownership stake in six racehorses and the venture had set up a series of adventures that brought several marvelous days at some famous racecourses.

I was smitten with the whole experience and now I was moving on, with a whole new focus of increasing my stake in just one racehorse and following 'my' horse over the course of a season. Previously I had been able to spread my interest over a number of horses over a couple of years. Although this was the 'thinnest' of all 'ownership' modes, it had the built in insurance that if one of the horses didn't do so well, then maybe one of the others would do better. Indeed this policy worked well in *'Four Hooves and a Prayer'*, because despite my miniscule stake I enjoyed some exciting days at the races with 'my' horses at Longchamps on Arc day, Haydock on Lancashire chase day and even into the winner's enclosure at Cartmel.

However, I realised that I'd been very lucky, a lot of this ownership was through racing club membership and I was competing with thousands of people to get to the races with 'my' horse. My tongue was placed firmly in cheek when I talked about 'owning my horse', I was fully aware that such 'ownership' was limited to the lucky day I made it to the races.

It was this motivation that made me consider taking the project a step further and making such 'ownership' a more tangible reality.

I would join a small syndicate in a horse, whereby I would increase my stake significantly and concentrate on just that horse for the season. Such a step would lack the insurance aspect that I had previously enjoyed, but would clearly be a more realistic model of racehorse ownership. This method would enable me to gain an insight into the day-to-day experiences of 'owning' a horse.

As one of a small number of people I would surely gain a more in depth experience of the realities of horse ownership. It would be a greater commitment on my part, both in terms of time and money but I hoped that it might bring greater rewards, not least in terms of the insight in concentrating on just one horse over a season.

So, the question was, where to start, on my new project of trying to bring about Prince Monolulu's famous line, 'I gotta horse'. In my previous ownership experiences, I had learnt that there was a vast profusion of horse racing syndicates out there. They are part of the great revolution that has swept through the sport in the last thirty years. Once the absolute preserve of the rich and landed gentry, horse racing partly out of necessity has reached out to the great unwashed and welcomed them into the sport as part of the democratisation of horse ownership.

One man's money it would seem is as good as the next's and although at the top end of the sport ownership remains in the exclusive grip of the super wealthy at the lower end of the scale there is now a range of opportunities for like minded people to group together and 'own' a horse through a syndicate.

There is a wide range of syndicates available to the public, and they vary greatly in terms of the kind of deals they can offer. I was now looking for a form of ownership that would allow me to see 'my' horse every time it ran.

This would necessitate joining a more 'bespoke' and smaller

grouping to allow myself such access. Such a situation would of course come with a higher price tag; the question was just how much was I prepared to spend to bring about my increased share percentage in a particular horse.

Previously my highest stake in an individual horse had been the 0.5% holding I had with the plucky Chilly Miss, and that had cost me £250. After due consideration, I felt that if this was going to be a 'meaningful' share in 'ownership' terms, then I should be looking to take up a 5% share. This would probably mean joining a syndicate of about twenty people.

In addition to a percentage share and price, there were a number of other factors that would help determine my final choice of horse.

Living in Manchester, I was hoping to find a partnership that would be as close to home as possible, but it immediately became apparent that such a geographical restriction would be difficult to bring about. Many of the likely syndicates seem to be located in the south. I decided therefore to extend the scope of my search, from Worcester in the south as far as the Scottish border in the north. Location can be an important factor for a number of reasons.

With a greater share in ownership, one could anticipate a higher number of stable visits; indeed some syndicates sell themselves on the basis of regular stable visits. Therefore it would be advantageous if one wasn't too far away from where the horse was stabled. Similarly, it was possible given transportation costs that the horse may not run too far away from its base.

This is an important consideration for the putative owner. When it comes to 'race day', you are never certain your horse will run until the declaration stage, which is normally the day before the race. It's even possible for your horse to be scratched on the day of the race itself, if it suffers a mishap or there is an extreme change in the going. On this basis it is obviously helpful if you don't live too far away from where the race will take place, so that you can move at short notice.

If for example Exeter was nominated as the race, but you weren't certain of participation until the day before, then you would be pushed to get to the race comfortably. I would hope that by choosing a trainer inside ones stipulated geographical area then this would limit this kind of problem arising. Unfortunately, my previous experiences told me that trainers could choose to race the horse 'anywhere'. Being a National Hunt fan, I knew I wanted a 'jumper', but I had no definite preference between a 'hurdler', or a 'chaser'. This would clearly be determined by what was available.

Of course I had my other sporting passions and indeed family commitments that might get in the way of this new horse project. In *"Four hooves and a Prayer"*, it was surprising how many times a horse run clashed with a 'home' football match or a family birthday. However, for the duration of this National Hunt season, I decided that the horse would come first and I would endeavour to see it every time it ran in a race.

Of the many existing syndicates, a couple took my eye and in stark contrast to Stan Hey and his pre Internet day searches, I was able to maximise information from that medium. There were lots of share options available, from two and a half percent to twenty five percent ownership packages, however I already knew that it was a five percent share I was interested in.

This would enable me to have a one twentieth share in the horse, ten times bigger than my previous largest 'ownership' share. One or two of the five percent models were available with what were clearly good horses.

Strictly speaking one could get involved with very exclusive partnerships such as the Million in Mind group, but the price tag of such deals are prohibitive. These horses are potentially top class jumpers, whose syndicates expect them to win races. There is even the possibility of selling a successful horse at the end of the season and recouping some of your investment. Such bespoke syndicates tend to quote prices on enquiry, but one can fairly assume the cost is in many thousands of pounds.

Axom, Elite's sister company offer similarly bespoke deals at the top end of the market, and they are often mailing to see if I am interested in taking up a share in one of their horses. These horses are nearly all well bred and in general their horses seem to run in some important races and sometimes win. However, although this project has moved away from the 'shoestring' days of *'Four Hooves and a Prayer'*, the prohibitive prices quoted were not the 'value' I had in mind. Some mid range syndicates tempt the eternal optimist in every potential 'owner', by talking in terms of unearthing the next Gold Cup winner. Once again you may spend a few thousand pounds discovering that particular fantasy is not going to happen.

One has to be realistic therefore when one is dealing with the 'value' end of the market. Wanting a five percent share in a horse and keeping to a budget of around a £1000, might be a difficult trick to pull off, but it was one that I was going to attempt. Clearly, at these prices I was not going to be taking a stake in the next Denman, but that didn't mean I couldn't achieve my overall objective in 'owning' the horse. In National Hunt one heard of occasional stories of a jewel being unearthed even at such modest prices. It could be a horse right at the start of a soon to be wonderful career, who will get his lucky 'owners' into the winners enclosure.

Realistic expectations are paramount, but an 'owner' should be allowed to dream, and sometimes dreams can come true.
After a few weeks of research I had narrowed the field down to

two syndicates. Both had horses in my price range, and appeared well run with good communications. One had the novel approach on focusing on the ethical status of horse ownership and they had a horse I was interested in that was apparently stabled in York. This horse was an experienced chaser, who had seen lots of racecourses but had rather less excursions to the winners enclosure. However, reading through his form figures he clearly possessed a certain durability and consistency. These are very important qualities at this end of the market because it infers that the animal is a tough character that will get you to the races on multiple occasions. When one is taking out a season only 'ownership' package, this is not to be sniffed at.

I was very interested and sent for the contract, but eventually two factors counted against this syndicate. Firstly the contract looked a little open ended, and although I could leave after the season, that wasn't their usual modus operandi. More tellingly, the trainer of the horse I had my eye on changed location, and although Durham was within my geographical area, it wasn't as close as York.

Instead I turned my attention to the Foxtrot syndicate. Their website had been very informative and their costing was fair and transparent. They had a string of horses and they appeared to be going through a purple patch with a 'strike rate' of over thirty percent.

As befits a successful syndicate their 'partnerships' seemed to sell out fast, and the website told me they only had shares available in a couple of horses.

One horse Midnight Silver seemed a particularly attractive proposition, a winning experienced chaser, and the only downside was his Southern location in Oxford. The other horse, Herefordshire, was in a much better location in Byton, Herefordshire, and was mysteriously an unraced seven year old, being promoted as a chaser to be trained by Kerry Lee. Herefordshire seemed to fit the bill perfectly. I had left my details with Foxtrot some weeks before and in one of those strange coincidental moments of fate I now received an email from them asking if I would be interested in this particular horse! Fate had indeed taken a hand, my detailed search was over, I emailed my acceptance and the 'I really gotta horse' project was underway.

## THE PARTNERSHIP

Foxtrot appeared to be a well-run efficient organisation and had quickly emailed me the contract and various details about the horse. The cost of £1250 was close enough to my target expenditure, and it didn't involve any vague notions of 'buying in'. This was a lease agreement, with a concrete start and end date, and I could see my maximum financial outlay from the outset. The lease agreement was between Foxtrot and Kerry Lee, as a member of the syndicate partnership I had brought about my genuine 'ownership' status, on terms I was very happy with.

 At five percent, it was by far my biggest share of ownership yet and although I was obviously putting in a lot more money than previously, I considered that overall I had obtained a good deal. This was 'real' ownership for the duration of the season.
It could even be argued that although it was costing me more money than previously, I was in fact, getting much better value. My previous biggest share with the Racegoers Club had after all been a 0.5% share for £250, therefore the equivalent here should have been £2500, I was therefore getting a better deal at half that amount.

 Dan was the syndicate manager and he seemed straightforward and approachable, sending all the pertinent information regarding 'my horse'. It was a couple of months later when on a stable visit a couple of the 'partners' told me that they just like myself had obtained the 'last share' in Herefordshire! Dan was clearly a good salesman, but true to his word the partnership had sold out very quickly, and I sent off the contract with my deposit cheque. As Dan said, this was indeed an exciting opportunity, a staying chaser with one of the country's up and coming trainers. It was time to bring out that most common of all clichés in this 'ownership' business, it was time to 'have a bit of fun' with our new horse.

My only slight reservation, at this stage, was the Foxtrot colours, which Herefordshire would race in. The sky blue silks were hardly close to my football allegiance, but the red hat made all the difference!

## THE HORSE

Breeding is very important in horse racing; supposedly it gives us an indication of how good our horse could be. Although not as important as on the flat, if the genes inherent in our horse (from the sire or the dam) are considered to be good ones, then hopefully our steed might have inherited some quality. *"Four Hooves and a Prayer"* showed that breeding is not an exact science, as the well-bred Geology proved to be a dud on the racecourse.

Non the less, at this stage if your horse comes from a top stallion, that can be considered a very positive start. In Herefordshire's case although his dam had never raced, his sire was the highly rated Beneficial. I dutifully did the research to see just what he might have passed onto our horse.

It transpired that Beneficial had been one of Irelands highest rated stallions and it would have cost a fair amount for the covering that produced Herefordshire. Beneficial had been a pretty good racehorse himself winning over six times and collecting over a quarter of a million pounds. I was becoming quite proficient at this breeding research, and I took note that

Beneficial's dam had won a French derby, so there was clearly speed and quality in the line that led to Herefordshire.

However competent Beneficial had been on the racecourse, he had really made his name and dictated a very profitable return for his owners as a stallion who had sired some top quality Irish National Hunt horses. He had sired 530 winners over the jumps, surely Herefordshire could add to the list. The list of his progeny was impressive, with top jumpers More of That, Beneficient and Cooldine amongst the horses. Cooldine had won at the Cheltenham festival, so it would seem that although Herefordshire was at the value end of the market, he did have some blue blood in his veins.

Of course Beneficial would have actually sired thousands of horses and many of them would according to the breeding law of averages have not amounted to much.

Non the less Beneficial kept his place as a leading sire by progeny earnings and was much in demand until he dropped dead (no doubt exhausted by his efforts!) in April 2013. There was a commercial tint to the mournful headline in the Racing Post: 'Beneficial dies…big loss to Irish racing'. He was twenty-three and had a full book of coverings due!
So it would seem that potentially, we might have a good horse on our hands. However, I was somewhat mystified as to how our horse had reached the age of seven but had never raced. The story was that someone in Ireland owned the horse but some form of mix up meant that a licence hadn't been obtained that would allow the horse to race. Of course these stories get taller with the telling, but it would appear Richard Lee saw the horse in a field, liked what he saw and bought the owner out and obtained the licence. The horse was now aged seven, and from my previous 'ownership' experiences, most jumpers would have gained experience in bumpers and hurdles races by that age.

However, it would seem that a different more relaxed route had been plotted for H, he had been allowed to mature and then this year had a couple of point to point races. This is effectively, steeple chasing for amateurs, and H had revealed his potential by winning one and being second in the other. We were therefore gaining a horse that was being specifically targeted at chases. By avoiding being flogged around hurdles courses he had not picked up any injuries and was therefore apparently in tip top physical condition.

## THE TRAINER

Kerry Lee was in only her second season as a trainer, having succeeded her father Richard, on his retirement. Richard was clearly still an important part of the set up and as we've seen had a fundamental role in Herefordshire's progress thus far. Clearly a 'horseman' of the old school, he was steeped in the experience of training for many years, having a particularly good record with chasers. As regards H, it would be fair to assume he knew a good chaser when he saw one. He had been the man in charge when H ran his two point to points. These races are regional affairs, run by the local hunt, jumping over the larger obstacles, albeit in relaxed smaller fields and could be seen as good practice for 'our boy'.

H had little problem with the fences, being second at North Ledbury and winning at Bitterley in April. I shocked my wife, by joining her on the weekly shop, in order to pick up a copy of Horse and Hound. She probably thought, given my recent fascination with horses that I had finally lost my marbles, as this would probably be the last magazine most people would imagine that I would purchase. There was however, reason for my madness, in that amongst the equestrian articles aimed at the 'country set', was a review of H's glorious point-to-point victories. Under the heading: 'Handy Herefordshire storms home', was an account that waxed lyrical on the horse's talents. Richard was quoted, claiming:' He's always jumped well, but we wanted to give him a nice introduction to his craft, which is why he's come point to pointing instead of being thrashed around a novice hurdle. He's certainly a promising one for the future'.

It was, it seemed, all coming together. H was a winter horse, which would relish softer ground, was eligible to run in novice chases straight away, and would be in the hands of the highly promising Kerry Lee.

Kerry had enjoyed a sensational debut season in 2015-16. She had done particularly well in chases, and had won a series of high profile televised races through that winter.

Russe Blanc and Top Gamble had won important races for her, but her major achievement was to win the Welsh Grand National with the veteran Mountainous. With a very impressive strike rate of over 27% with her chasers, we could not really have had our horse in any better hands. I was pleased that H was going to a relatively small stables (of approximately thirty horses) on this basis I considered he would receive greater individual attention.

Initially news of Kerry and our horse was through Dan's email reports that began to appear in September. It was quite amusing, as Dan appeared to be hitting the double prompt with every email, as they always appeared twice. It was a case of Dan Dan the syndicate man, as a nod to Charles Hawtrey's thankfully brief cameo as "Dan Dan' in the much underrated film, 'Carry on Screaming'. Whether one read the email once or twice, the inference of these first reports was that Herefordshire had settled well, but there would be no rush to the racecourse. He was enjoying his work on the gallops but Kerry wanted softer ground before she started to school him over fences.

There was even talk at this stage of visits by the chiropractor, to straighten out all those important limbs. No stone it would seem was left unturned to see our boy in perfect condition by the time he did go racing. This it would seem might be some time off, but we were informed that there was some tentative race plans for six weeks time.

Clearly one had to be patient with 'our' promising horse. Despite a natural desire to see the horse race as soon as possible, all key decisions were always in the hands of the trainer. When everything was ready then we would be off to the races.

In the meantime we had to content ourselves with schooling reports and the news that we would be able to see the horse and trainer on a stable visit near the end of October. The time seemed apposite to review just what I expected from the next seven months of 'real ownership'.

## HOPES and ASPIRATIONS

So by mid September we were all set for a hopefully successful chasing season with 'our' horse. The syndicate 'partnership' was set up to my satisfaction. The 'partners' looked like they had obtained a potentially good horse and we had a trainer with the perfect profile to bring the best out of our chaser.

What could possibly go wrong? Well in the horse racing game, just about anything! Whether it is the horse, the weather, the ground, the trainer's form, I was well versed in the potential mishaps. Non the less at the outset of the 'I really gotta horse' project I was quietly pleased with myself and felt it only appropriate to set myself some targets over the next seven months:

• That I would endeavour to see my horse run in all his races. This can be surprisingly difficult to achieve, when race-days clash with family functions or some of my other sporting commitments. However, given the trouble and expense I had gone to, I decided that the horse would come first. After all for the first time in my 'ownership' history I would now be guaranteed owner tickets for every race. It would be wasteful if I didn't take up my full allocation.

• Horses can be very fragile creatures and it can be tempting fate to specify how many races in the season, I would be satisfied with. I had known some horses who were constantly visiting the vet and even some who never raced in the allocated season. However, at this stage I considered that if 'our' horse ran half a dozen races over the season, then this could be considered very satisfactory.

• No one should go into horse 'ownership' thinking that they might make money. My earlier experiences, over the last four years, are that the prize money is miserly. Of course I now owned a bigger stake in the horse and would correspondingly expect a higher return. As a general rule of thumb, the 'owner' can expect to pick up approximately 75% of any prize money, with the trainer and the jockey collecting the rest. Although I was dealing in the 'value' end of the market, and my horse was hardly likely to be competing for any blue riband events, one still had to have aspirations to win a race. I therefore set myself the target of a win and some places in the races my horse competed in. Call me an optimist (and not many people do!), but I was quite lucky with my previous 'ownership' capers, so therefore I didn't consider this target to be impossible.

• A really important aspiration is that your horse will bring you to some of the great National Hunt Racecourses around Britain. Again this is determined to some extent by how good your horse is. While I knew Herefordshire was not going to be gracing the Cheltenham festival, I hadn't ruled out the possibility that he might feature at one of their minor meetings. There were lots of other nice courses near the Lees stables, so visits to Ludlow, Warwick and Chepstow were high on my wish list. Given the horse's name, I was almost certain that he would end up at the newly re-opened Hereford racecourse.

• Lastly, of course one wanted to see Herefordshire get safely through the season without injury, mishap or something even worse!

If he finished the season safe and sound, with an impressive BHA rating we would all consider it to be a success. So with all these hopes in mind, it was time to see what the next seven months had in store, as I set off on my taste of 'real' horse ownership.

# CHAPTER 2
# OCTOBER 2016

**Sunday 2ⁿᵈ October**

October was turning out to be a very quiet month on the horse 'owning' front as the partners had to content themselves with one or two relatively brief communication lines from Kerry. The general message was that H was now cantering and generally doing everything that was asked of him. There was clearly no rush to see a racecourse at this stage in proceedings.

I was fairly relaxed about this state of affairs, as otherwise I might have fallen at the first fence in my initial aim of managing to attend every race. The potential dilemma was that my better half and myself had booked some autumnal sun in Lisbon, until the tenth of October. I was firmly of the opinion that I wouldn't get a sympathetic hearing if I proposed any late swap to take in a race at Hereford!

**Tuesday 11ᵗʰ October**

We are enjoying an Indian summer, but the dry autumnal weather seems to have put all potential racing plans on permanent hold.

**Wednesday 12ᵗʰ October**

It's getting closer to my annual visit to beautiful Ludlow with Mr J and Mr T. We have been on this cultural visit now for the past few years, taking in a challenging walk, the excellent local beers and rounding off the trip with a visit to Ludlow races.

I noticed that the planned stable visit at nearby Byton was on Friday of the same week. My recommendation to add on an extra day to the trip was gratefully accepted by the others and Dan as efficient as ever allocated a couple of guest tickets for the stable visit.

Given the dry weather and the lack of any concrete racing plans, I didn't suppose that there was any chance of seeing H race at Ludlow, but wouldn't it be great if he did.

## Sunday 16th October

Final details are coming through from Foxtrot in terms of the arrangements for next week's stable visit. It would appear that usually new 'partnerships' start with a dinner on the same day as the stable visit, but this will not be the case this year. Apparently the reason is that racing is on at Cheltenham and various 'partners' want to go racing straight after the visit.

There is apparently some possibility that H might make his debut at Hereford at the end of the month. However, this seems tentative at best, and given that we are still enjoying the sunshine, I am not over optimistic of this coming about. No doubt we will know a bit more when we speak to the trainer at the stable visit.

## Friday 21st October
## The Stable Visit

Byton, on the English side of the Welsh border is a strikingly beautiful location. We are blessed with a sunny day, which might be a negative in terms of racing plans but still allows for a wonderful backdrop to the stable visit. This North-western part of Herefordshire contains the black and white village trail and we drive through these characteristic black and white timber-framed buildings and their churches, reminders of the long history of this area. We make our way up to Brand Hill, just half a mile from the Lees stable. Here in spectacular autumn colours is a stiff well-appointed gallops. We've arrived early, but we are soon joined by what is a good turn out of about twenty-five people.
Stable visits are a very important part of the 'ownership' game and are promoted by Foxtrot.

They are a chance for the 'partners' to see how the horse is training and discuss all aspects of progress and planning with your trainer. The 'partners' seem a nice bunch of people, although initially we are all strangers to one another, but the conversation will quickly gravitate to the one thing we've got in common, our horse. The 'partners' seem to be a mix of race-going boys and a smattering of the country set. Richard arrives in some sort of four by four, and starts the process of ferrying people up the hill towards the top of the gallops. In keeping with our weekly endeavours, we decide to walk up the quarter mile accent to the top of the hill. Once we have all assembled at the top, Kerry arrives in a similar vehicle to her dad's.

It's a relatively informal gathering, and we wander around training our binoculars on the bottom of the hill, from where we expect H to emerge. Kerry finally calls us together to make a brief introduction. She appears slightly nervous, she is a new trainer and this syndicate partnership is probably an innovative venture for the yard. She explains that H will lead another five horses up a couple of circuits of the gallops and then we will come together for a more detailed discussion.

H led the other horses from the shadows at the bottom of the hill up the gallops and into the brilliant sunshine at the top of the hill. To my eyes he did it impressively, moving fluently at a good pace, he was a strong athletic looking horse.

Mr T, a fine judge of these things, was most impressed. He was particularly taken by the fact that the exertions seemed to have taken so little out of H. Mr J, circulating in his usual discrete fashion, thought my fellow 'owners', were suitably impressed.

As the 'partners' gathered around the horse, taking copious photographs of H, Kerry began to outline her thoughts on 'our' horse. Once more she emphasised that he was a winter horse, which would be seen to best effect when the mud was flying in January.

Non the less she claimed he was race fit now and if some rain appeared we would be off to the races. She clearly liked the horse, and felt he was capable of good things, which I took to mean, important races in the future. On questioning she affirmed he was a particularly good jumper and that the obstacles were not going to be a problem. Circumspectly, she added that with all horses, you never know how good they are, until they appear on the racecourse.

Conscious of the Indian summer weather, I asked her just how important was the going, given that his two point to point runs had been on good going. That was a 'different kind of racing', she retorted, and explained that it was his galloping action that determined a preference for soft ground. It was finally mooted after much discussion that a race at Hereford at the end of the month, might well be his debut run. This was music to my ears, this would be Hereford's second meeting since it reopened, and I had never visited the track. Apparently there was a three-mile beginners chase on the thirty-first, which Kerry thought might be an ideal starting point. Given that was ten days away, one could only hope that the unpredictable British climate would oblige.

The ongoing Indian summer was part of the conversation when we all reconvened on the Lees veranda, some time later. Generous light refreshment was delivered, Mr J possibly giving away his Oxford University background, was particularly impressed with the quiche. Mr T, tucked into the pies.

Race entries are completed five days before a particular race, so there was much conversation regarding how likely a runner H might be at his namesake course. One or two thought this extremely unlikely, whereas others stuck to the optimistic line that weather forecasts can be wrong. Surprisingly the Lees didn't take the chance to parade their stable stars, a missed opportunity I would say.

Instead I wandered down to the stable area to see H who had

returned from his morning exertions. He is a horse with a friendly, relaxed temperament. I'm not sure if this tells us anything about his innate racing ability, but it certainly makes for a successful photo-shoot.

**Wednesday 26th October**
Potentially very good news as H is one of fifteen entries for the beginners chase at Hereford on the last day of the month. I am mildly surprised by the news, as there is no change in the weather, but know enough to realise that this doesn't mean he will definitely run. It is a race for four year olds and upwards, who have not won a chase race, and does look a nice place for H to start.

As it is potentially such an important race for 'our' horse, I dutifully check out the competition. It is the usual mix of yards and types, some high profile yards, some experienced horses, some summer jumpers and some about to start the winter season. I note that Paul Nichols has entered a Sir Alex Ferguson owned horse, now that would be an interesting mix of 'owners'!

**Thursday 27th October**
I peruse the Foxtrot email sent last night, trying to work out just how likely a run could be. Race entries cost money, and although this is a moderate amount for a race of this kind, one could claim that it means the trainer is seriously considering the race. The Foxtrot line is this is a competitive race, on ground that is considered less than ideal and this naturally dampens my enthusiasm. However, optimism is restored by the last part of the message that reiterates that Kerry is keen to get a 'run into him', and that the experience would leave him 'spot on', when the soft ground finally arrives. Suitably emboldened, I begin to make tentative enquiries into a trip to Hereford.

**Saturday 29ᵗʰ October**

The high-pressure system that has brought us such stable warm weather remains intact, and no rain is forecast for the next few days. It might be a question of just how keen Kerry is to race or doing a last minute rain dance.

**Sunday 30ᵗʰ October**

I scan the Racing Post website for the declarations for the race at Hereford mid morning, but no news is announced and the list of the original entries remains intact. Further checks are unnecessary as shortly afterwards I receive an email that tells me that H has not been declared to race, due to the 'ground'. The rest of the email is short and to the point, claiming the horse is ready to run but will 'wait for some rain', before further running plans are announced.

 There is no getting away from it this is disappointing news. Although the weather had showed no sign of change, I did think the trainer was moving towards taking a chance on running H. It is a frustrating situation for the 'partnership', we have been in operation for over a month, and a run at this stage would have been just about perfect. It's a dilemma for the syndicate, they have paid good money and I am sure want to see the horse run. At the same time they realise the risks involved and I'm sure wouldn't want to see the horse injured, as that would obviously cause a much greater delay in terms of the season.

 In matters of this kind we all must be guided by the trainer, the trainer is always right and her decision is final!

# CHAPTER 3
# November 2016

**Sunday 6 November**
The dry weather keeps up and there is still no sign of a run and
nothing seems to be planned either. My bank statement shows
that my second direct debit payment has been made to Foxtrot.

However, the wider racing news puts my immediate travails into
a truer context. Freddy Tyliki, the flat jockey who has ridden
many Elite horses particularly for James Fanshawe, is involved in
a terrible pile up at Kempton and is left paralysed in the lower
half of his body.

 On the equine front, the great Irish chaser Vautour has been put
down after a freak training mishap and on the same day Nicky
Henderson's Simonsig sustains a fatal injury racing at
Cheltenham.

**Friday 11 November**
Finally, some positive news. Kerry is planning Herefordshire's
debut in earnest it would seem, as news filters through on three
'suitable' race options. Wetherby on the twenty third of the month
or Ffos Las on the thirtieth. There is even talk of a follow up race
at Hereford in Christmas week.

 This is more like it, I'd be happy with either venue and I am
particularly attracted by the possibility of a trip to Hereford in
Christmas week. I think my better half will be keen on a trip to the
Cathedral City and a stop over to see the Mappa Mundi.
 One must not get carried away, the first issue is to get H out on
the racecourse for his belated debut and the really important news
is that it has started to rain properly for the first time in weeks. It's

funny how this ownership lark can influence ones outlook on life, normally I would delight in the dry bright autumn we have enjoyed, instead it's the previous week's rain dance that is being thanked.

**Friday 18 November**
Herefordshire who is apparently schooling well has been entered at Wetherby. It's a three-mile novice chase and there are seventeen horses entered. Kerry is perusing them, but they look pretty good to me, some with high hurdle ratings and a couple that have already won a chase race. A decision will be made next Tuesday, but the management sound a little doubtful.

**Tuesday 22 November**
Its declaration day, but Kerry has decided to swerve the race. She seems to have been put off by the experience of the opposition. In actual fact, only five horses are declared, although they do include odds on favourite, Zeroshadesofgrey.

It's a shame, Wetherby was just an hour away, I fancied Herefordshire and its been bucketing it down, leading to an official description of the going as 'soft'. Ideal conditions I would have thought, but the trainer is the boss.

Hindsight is a wonderful thing.

**Friday 25 November**
News comes through that Herefordshire has indeed been entered for a class four beginners' chase at Ffos Las at the end of the month. Given that Kerry avoided Wetherby (where the odds on favourite got turned over and only three horses finished), I feel that we may be declared this time.

There are eighteen horses entered and again they look an experienced bunch, with some big stables running quality hurdlers who they hope will make a successful transition to chasing.

**Sunday 27 November**
Kerry is 'keen' to run H. He has been moving well on the gallops and all the connections are hopeful that he will do himself justice on his belated racecourse debut. Recent communications though have sounded a note of caution, if he is declared, the partners should have realistic expectations of our horse, and it is after all his first racecourse appearance.

**Tuesday 29 November**
The day has finally come. Some three months after joining the partnership Herefordshire will make his debut at Ffos Las, tomorrow.

 The Sporting Life reported that there will be seven horses declared for the 2.20 Beginners Chase over two miles seven furlongs at the south Wales course. The highly rated Nichols' horse is gone, but Mr McManus has two horses that have won at Cheltenham running and with Peter Bowen also having a couple of runners, it looks like a tough baptism for H.

 Well of course our 'boy', could be 'anything' as they say and on that basis we can maintain the optimism that all owners presumably have until the reality of the race day appears.
I'm just happy that we are finally going racing and although it's to deepest South Wales, one consolation is that it's my old mate Les Taylors patch and he has kindly agreed to pick me up at Abergavenny station and drive us to the course.

 Needless to say, the weather has changed back to cold clear dry conditions. This means that H's preferred soft going is unlikely and indeed with the temperatures set to plummet overnight I am slightly concerned that we will get any racing at all.

 However, when I ring the course they seem sanguine enough, no inspection is planned and we are all systems go for Herefordshire's debut.

\*     \*     \*

## RACEDAY-HEREFORDSHIRE AT FFOS LAS,
**Wednesday, 30 November**
**The Racecourse**

I was still concerned about racing prospects as the train from Manchester rattled past a Ludlow racetrack that looked like a winter wonderland. However, by the time Les picked me up the sun was melting away the frost as we made our way through the famous Welsh valleys.

An argument could be made that Ffos Las is Britain's newest racecourse, if one takes into account older courses that close and then reopen. Opening on the eighteenth of June 2009, it was the first racecourse to be built in the UK for eighty years. Built on the site of an open cast coal mine, it was Wales's third racecourse. Located near Llanelli in rugby country, the course has that new planned look. Its in a natural amphitheatre, some twelve furlongs in length and it seemed quite a flat landscape, making me wonder if it would suit H, who I somehow see as being well suited by a demanding hilly course, dare I say, like Wetherby.

The owner's facilities were at first sight somewhat basic, as we passed through a portacabin located on the edge of a car park. However, once onto the course the owner's bar and restaurant were spick and span and the meet and greet lady gave us both a warm welcome to the racecourse.

She seemed particularly impressed that I had travelled down from Manchester, as I proudly announced we were here to watch Kerry Lee's horse. Once ensconced, we were able to partake of the excellent complimentary Welsh cakes and tea and coffee. On going for a walk around the course, I was surprised to see that they didn't seem to have any wifi or the large TV screens that are highly visible at all British race courses. Still, on the flat panorama that that lay in front of me, I should be able to get a clear view of proceedings.

*     *     *

**PRERACE**
As the first races unfolded, I ran into a couple of the 'partners' and very soon we began to discuss what we thought of H's chances for the afternoon. There was a consensus that this was a tough baptism. H was possibly between the rock and a hard place. If he ran well against horses that were on high BHA marks in the 130's, this would mean that he would subsequently be in line for a good mark himself and a corresponding weight. However, if he didn't run well, then all that optimism that the Lees might have a really good horse would be somewhat punctured.

The opposition certainly looked stiff. The McManus horses Call the Cops trained by Nicky Henderson and Join the Clan trained by Jonjo O'Neill had Cheltenham form and were at the top of the betting boards. Call the Cops had won the Pertemps final at Cheltenham in 2015 and had an impressive BHA rating of 148; at 13/8 he was a warm favourite. Join the Clan had run at the festival in March and boasted a BHA mark of 135, at 7/4 he had also attracted plenty of support.

Watching both go around the pre parade ring, Les reckoned he didn't think too much of the Henderson horse and there were mutterings regarding the fact that this was now chasing, so maybe those high ratings wouldn't count for so much.

With Land of Vic dropping out, there were only six horses going to post, but with the wily Peter Bowen's Pearl Swan and Paul Morgan's West Wizard in the opposition, I had the increasing feeling that H was going to do well just to manage a place.

Kerry wasn't in attendance today, and it was her father Richard that greeted us. He maintained the mantra that he didn't know what to expect, which was fair enough given that H had never been on a racecourse before.

Having said that, they clearly liked this horse, he had been working well at home and he certainly looked the part as he strode around the parade ring. Jamie Moore now arrived from the weighing room tipping his cap and cheerfully introducing himself.

Jamie from the Moore racing dynasty, was well versed in the meeting and greeting of connections, and jauntily took up his station, friendly and upbeat.

He often rides for Kerry and he had been up on H in the past, pronouncing himself impressed with the horse and made it clear that he would go along with the pace and see what happened. "We're looking for a nice introduction', he surmised, "If we get in a winning position we'll see what happens". Richard was more circumspect, 'get him jumping well and lets get round', he countered. Once the pleasantries were completed Jamie was given the leg up and off they went for the start. The moment was now upon us, all these months of waiting to see what kind of horse we had would soon be revealed, he was up against it, new to the game, but when a horse hasn't run competitively before there is always the thought, he 'could be anything'. I had no trouble finding odds of 20/1 and suitably emboldened I placed a tenner each way, you never know.

*     *     *

## THE RACE - BEGINNERS' STEEPLECHASE (CLASS FOUR) 3 MILES

The race began and indeed continued at a very sedate pace and initially H settled in second position behind Pearl Swann. His jumping looked good, deliberate but clean; of course as they were dawdling around the course he seemed to have plenty of time to see his fences.

As they finished the first circuit, the position of the horses didn't change much and neither did the pace. This was a tactical race with Peter Bowen's horse cleverly dictating the pace, Jamie Moore later confided that at this point he was minded to inject some pace and take the lead, but with it being Herefordshire's debut he wasn't sure if that would have been a good idea.

Halfway around the second circuit, Pearl Swann finally made a move and increased the pace, with West Wizard and Hurricane Girl setting off in pursuit. H though seemed stuck in the same groove and quickly became detached from the leading group and then fell behind the McManus duo to find himself in last place.

The race was over, but stoically H continued to plug on and surprisingly at the last fence, Call the Cops the pre race favourite refused and H jumped the fence to wander home in fifth place. Pearl Swann having 'made all' won the race, but the favoured McManus pair disappointed with Join the Clan a well beaten fourth and Call the Cops refusing at the last and unseating his rider.

It was an underwhelming start to Herefordshire's racing career, the Racing Post summed the performance up succinctly: "tracked leader to second, stayed prominent until lost place 10th, behind from 14, tailed off".

*    *    *

## POSTRACE

My immediate reaction was that this was a disappointing start for H, and that night's perusal of the term 'tailed off' taken together with being beaten by a distance of fifty-five lengths was I considered somewhat telling.

But back in the pre parade ring things were more up beat. Jamie Moore had dismounted with Richard Lee and the 'partners' looking on. The jockey thought H had 'done alright', he had kept going, 'he's got the feel of a dour stayer', he ventured. Richard checked on his jumping, 'no problem, he can jump a fence' said Jamie.

The mood had visibly picked up amongst the 'partners'. The race had been run all wrong for our boy and overall this was valuable experience was the consensus. Richard became almost animated as he talked about going to war with H, once he had run three times and got a handicap mark. When the mud was deep in January and February that's when we would see the best of our racehorse. 'Kerry's horses always need their first run' opined one of the partners. It was onwards and upwards, or so it seemed.

I thought about this positive spin on the long train journey back home. I had enough experience of this horse owning lark to know that it certainly wasn't about a regular procession to the winner's enclosure each time you go racing. We were at the 'value' end of horse ownership, so our expectations had to be realistic. There are no guarantees in racing, even Mr McManus's millions had come up short here, with arguably his two horses doing worse than the inexperienced Herefordshire. *"Four Hooves and a Prayer"* had taught me that for every day at Longchamp you might have five days down the field at Catterick.

However, to some extent the bubble had burst at Ffos Las, H was no longer the unknown 'could be anything' racehorse, he had now run and reality could set in. I had actually thought H's run somewhat underwhelming and Dan's email that night was more in line with this view. H was never likely to make an impact on horses with such high BHA grades, he will have learnt a lot but it would seem that little could be expected until he had been handicapped.

 Non the less having safely navigated his first race, it was now surely safe to go ahead and book the hotel in Hereford for December the 19th. A real Christmas treat and no doubt an opportunity for H to seek redemption at the appropriately named racecourse.

# CHAPTER 4
# DECEMBER 2016

**Thursday 1ˢᵗ December**
Kerry reports that H is fine the day after his exertions, he has sustained a minor cut, but it is nothing to worry about. Optimism is fully returning now, as someone seems to have picked up on the television commentator Luke Harvey's comment that H apparently looked a good prospect.

**Sunday 11ᵗʰ December**
H has been fine all week, doing some light work and the very positive news is that he is 'very likely to run' at Hereford on Monday week. This is really good news as I can plan the Hereford trip and look out for the five day entries next week.

**Monday 12ᵗʰ December**
Disaster! News comes through that H has sustained an injury and the Hereford race is off. Apparently the horse was found to be lame following a piece of quicker work on the gallops this morning. He would appear to have sustained a tendon injury, which appears quite a serious diagnosis to me, and this is confirmed by the additional news that his season is over! Foxtrot and Kerry Lee concur that this is very disappointing news, but that is a massive understatement.

One has to be pragmatic in these situations, I know enough about the game to know that these or worse things can happen to your horse. Over the last three seasons I had been lucky that none of my chosen horses sustained an injury on this scale. Of course the horse's welfare comes first, but H would be nine years old next season and despite the Lees positive views about a return to the racecourse, I was less sure. So all those weeks of waiting for the winter rains had come to nothing and seeing H at Hereford in Christmas week was not to be, maybe those sky blue colours were unlucky after all!

Now of course the 'partnership' was left without a horse, but before I could look into the financial implications of that, I noted that in the same communication it was proposed that the 'partners' would be given a 'replacement' horse. Dan the syndicate manager was of the opinion that this was a good offer and would allow us to have an instant replacement that could run in January. This horse was an unraced four year old, tentatively named Sonshine. He was a store horse, which I believe means he was bought to be kept to one side and raced in the future. It would appear that his moment had come; in a dramatic day it was a question of out with the old, and in with the new!

**Tuesday 13ᵗʰ December**
After yesterday's dramatic news I began to sift through the information I had on the 'new' horse. Kerry's dad had bought him at the derby sales in Ireland eighteen months ago as a store horse, and he had developed quickly into an imposing horse of over sixteen hands. The Lees were very enthusiastic about him, considering him to be a smart animal with a big future ahead of him.

His breeding still had a link to the sire Beneficial, but this time it was less direct as that horse had sired Sonshine's dam, Good Shine. She had been mated with Dubai Destination to produce Sonshine in 2012. Dubai Destination lacked Beneficial's National Hunt kudos, but he had enjoyed success on the racecourse and as a breeding stallion.

There was no getting away from the fact that this was a very different deal from the one that I had signed up for.
Initial thoughts centred on going with a mature Kerry Lee chaser who had been spared flogging himself around hurdles and would

be ready to excel in chases in the winter months. Now we were going racing with an unproven four year old, targeting bumper races with the hope that we might be hurdling before the end of the lease.

Still, we were where we were, all our hopes were transferred onto the 'new' horse, a rendition of Morecambe and Wise's theme tune seemed appropriate, maybe our new boy would bring us sunshine in 2017.

**FRIDAY 16<sup>th</sup> December**

Apparently Sonshine is only a temporary moniker and invitations are now invited from the 'partners' to name our new steed.

This usually means trawling through sire and dam family names, trying to find something appropriate and at the same time making sure the new name hasn't already been taken. Given that Arkle and Denman were non-starters I forwarded the opinion that I liked Sonshine and was happy to stay with that.

**FRIDAY 23<sup>rd</sup> December**

The horse is to be called, Destined To Shine. This seems a bit long-winded to me and one could say either reflects a healthy dose of optimism or maybe become a hostage to fortune. Non-the less this is to be the name and it's growing on me already.

However, for the sake of brevity I will now refer to it as DTS.

# 2017

## CHAPTER 5
## JANUARY

**Sunday 1st January**

A New Year is always a time of fresh hopes expectations and good resolutions. It's no different with horses and taking stock of the old year there was room for improvement in the "I really gotta a horse' project. Recent months had been more like the experiences of Mr Hey (who indirectly had set these ownership capers up by the frustrating experiences he recounted in 'An Arm and Four Legs'). His horses barely saw the racecourse or if they eventually did, little joy was to be had.

The last three months had seen just one underwhelming racecourse performance by the unfortunate Herefordshire to be followed shortly after by injury and potential retirement. This was not much of a return for the increased financial investment on my part and summed up what a hard sport horse racing can be.

Foxtrot as a whole were doing well with a series of impressive winners and a remarkable strike rate over the last twelve months, unfortunately H wasn't able to add to their tally.

Still we had a new horse and the news today was that DTS could make his debut in just two weeks time. He was considered something of a baby but it was felt that getting him out onto a racecourse would be a positive experience for him.

## Wednesday 4th January

News comes through that Kerry is considering the bumper race at Warwick in ten days time. This sounds positive news, I've never been to Warwick and the meeting is one of their highlight jumping days of the year.

## Thursday 5th January

DTS apparently did a 'bit of work' (practice) at Bangor on Dee racecourse yesterday. This was to give him some experience of a racecourse on a race day and seems a good idea to me. He went through the saddling up, saw the crowds and even had champion jockey Richard Johnson on board for a gallop. Richard liked the way the horse moved but unfortunately he has questioned whether the horse would be ready for Warwick. This is a blow, after recent months there is a slight impatience to see a horse on a racecourse. However, Kerry hasn't immediately ruled Warwick out and instead wants to see how DTS handles the next few days. Southwell at the end of the month has been mooted as a replacement venue if DTS doesn't make Warwick.

## Sunday 8th January

Still no news on whether DTS will take up the Warwick option, and I'm not very optimistic. At least the weather remains very mild for this time of year. This can be a major consideration for us horse owners! Given the frustrations of the previous months all I need now is the three month big freeze that the Daily Express annually threatens its readers with.

## Tuesday 10th January

DTS has been entered at Warwick, which is pleasing news but comes with the caveat that Kerry still wants to do one more piece of work before declaring our horse. I'm quite surprised really; I thought the comments of Richard Johnson had probably done for Warwick.

For the first time in a long time I'm able to go to the Racing Post site and examine the entries for the 4.05 two mile flat race at Warwick. There are thirty-three of them and the usual mix of strong stables and well related horses abound. Non-the less, just having an entry seems a positive development after recent tribulations.

**Thursday 12th January**
News filters through that DTS will be declared tomorrow. This is great news and quite a relief. Presumably, DTS has done well in his schooling and Kerry it would seem is happy for him to take his place at Warwick. She thinks it is going to be a 'hot' bumper but hopes the horse can do himself justice.

 It looks a great card at Warwick featuring their Betfred Classic Chase, so we should be guaranteed a great day's racing what ever happens.

**Friday 13th January**
I check the Racing Post declarations at lunchtime and DTS is listed along with fifteen other horses. Given that this a 'bumper' race (a flat race under National Hunt rules for beginners) we haven't got any 'form' to guide us in terms of the opposition. Usually the cost of the horse or whether it is related to previous winners is something of an indication, but not always an accurate guide.

 The racing trade papers are usually full of terms like, 'one for the shortlist', 'highly respected' or 'superbly bred', but the truth of the matter is no one really knows, until we see the horse perform. DTS is listed as an 18,000-euro purchase, but there were some in the field that cost three times that sum. Tizzard, Greatrex and Skelton were represented, although the combination of Fry and Fehily on Dollnamix were likely to be favourites. The horse Kaveman, seemed the biggest threat to me, he was related to Ballyandy who had won the Cheltenham bumper last year so had the breeding, as they say. More pertinently, Gary Moore trained him, and unfortunately it transpired that this meant his son the jockey Jamie Moore wouldn't be available for us, but would be riding for his dad.

Our jockey was to be Robbie Dunne, I knew little about him, but the next days Racing Post had a small feature claiming he was having something of a breakthrough season.

The weather, which naturally had suddenly become much colder once we had declared, might have been a concern if it were not for Warwick racecourse covering the track for the last three days and making certain that tomorrows racing would go ahead. We were all set now for the belated second race day and the DTS debut.

*     *     *

## RACEDAY – DESTINED TO SHINE AT WARWICK, SATURDAY, 14th JANUARY
## THE RACECOURSE

If getting the horse onto a racecourse has been something of a problem, the same cannot be said about my transportation to the courses, as once again the rail connections worked superbly. From Manchester via Crewe and Leamington Spa all the trains ran on time and delivered Sue and myself to Warwick rail station by noon.

In something of a moment of déjà vu we sat in the very same ornate waiting room at Leamington Spa that Stan Hey had waxed lyrically about in his book. Not being sure how close we were to the course we took a reasonably priced taxi, which delivered us directly to the impressive owners entrance.

The 'Course inspector' had once talked about Warwick traditionally having a reputation of a course that was 'hard to love', but that was obviously a long time ago. I may have been slightly influenced by the prosecco being proffered as we moved through reception and indeed the free meal vouchers handed out by the cheerful receptionists, but my impressions were immediately positive ones.

 There was still rain in the air as we walked briskly past the spacious pre parade and parade rings. We were ushered into the owners and trainers building, which were predictably bustling with today's 'connections' on what would have been one of Warwick's most important race days in the year. The food on offer maintained my sense of joie de vie, this was no standard biscuits and tea operation, but local well made pies adorned by mashed potatoes and fresh vegetables. Above this building is a small viewing gallery that allows a clear view of the gently undulating finishing straight.

 I decided to have a walk after this pleasant lunch and away to my right was the main stand and in the distance views of the town and the church of St Mary's.

 I watched the first couple of races from the main stand, where the recently deposed Jim McGrath (channel four racing had just lost the television rights to ITV, and McGrath was one of their stalwart commentators), watched in silence.

 Although it was over fifteen years since the 'Course inspector' had visited, one characteristic feature of the course remained and that was the hill that obscured the view as the horses disappeared to the right of the main stand. Lee had amusingly referred to old legend indicating that all sorts of malpractice used to occur before the mobile cameras kept the horses and their jockeys in view.

 The horses as in time in memorial would follow the undulations behind the hill to emerge jumping some stiff fences before battling out a challenging slightly uphill finish. This was a proper steeple-chasing course and although DTS was not jumping any fences today, I was grateful to him that he had brought me to a racecourse for which I developed an instant liking.

**PRERACE**

I ran into a couple of Foxtrot members before the racing and all agreed that this was a good race meeting to choose for the 'partners' second race day. By the time we collected in the parade ring before DTS appeared there must have been twenty members assembled, I don't know how Dan does it. The pre race official line to the partners was that expectations were limited, mainly due to the unknown quality of our steed, this being his first appearance on a racecourse.

Kerry Lee had been delayed from meeting us as in the previous race, the showpiece Classic Chase she had saddled three runners. In a predictable show of support for 'our' trainer some of us had backed her horses and in my case Good To Know had rewarded my each way enterprise with an impressive second place. So we were in good cheer when she eventually met up with us in the parade ring.

She seemed brisk and to the point, she was pleased with DTS but wanted to see how he would cope with a proper race-day. Jamie Moore wasn't with us today, but I could see him in the parade ring, he was riding for his dad aboard the favourite Kaveman.
Our jockey for the day was Robbie Dunne, who I knew little about, other than he was a young aspiring jockey that by chance also featured in a Racing Post feature on his association with the horse Rigadin De Beauchene.

They too had run in the classic, with the veteran horse proving a handful, ejecting the jockey in the preliminaries and then tearing into a big lead in the actual race before not surprisingly fading. Robbie seemed non-the worse for his experiences and touched his cap in response to the good wishes.

As usual there was an intense tête-à-tête between trainer and jockey before Robbie mounted DTS and set off for the start. Expectations seemed genuinely modest as we made our separate ways to the stands. The bumper (named thus because such inexperienced animals often bump into each other when running) is the last race on the card and is often the cue for a mass evacuation of the punters as they make their way for a swift exit. However, that was not the case today, the parade ring had been full and the stands seemed likewise. The viewing gallery in the owners stand was still packed, with quite a few of the 'partners' in attendance as we trained our binoculars on the horses in the middle distance. A race past four o clock on a January afternoon can be a gloomy affair, but not today, visibility was totally clear as fourteen horses were corralled at the start.

*     *     *

## THE RACE - STANDARD OPEN NATIONAL HUNT FLAT RACE (CLASS 6), 2 MILES

The race set off at a steady pace, DTS pulling slightly seemed keen to show what he could do. Robbie tried to keep a keen hold on him but eventually allowed the horse to bowl along towards the front of affairs. Indeed for much of the race DTS appeared to be going well, alternating between second and third place.

As they turned the final bend and made towards the finish DTS seemed to be holding his position but the rest of the field were gathered menacingly just behind him. His earlier efforts seemed to have tired him and he faded over the last three furlongs to finish tenth of the fourteen runners.

As if to show how random bumper races can be, Tim Vaughan's Point of Principle was the 50/1 winner and the fancied co favourite Kaveman was back in sixth place.

                    *       *       *

## POSTRACE

 A slightly subdued group of partners made their way down the
steps of the stand. The light was fading now and some 'partners'
made their way onto the course in an attempt to see the response
of jockey and trainer, while others returned to the warmth of the
owner's bar.

When many of us met up in the bar, the initially muted response
of 'partners', no doubt influenced by the fade out, was now
predictably moving towards a more upbeat assessment. This was
an encouraging debut appeared to be the consensus; DTS had
shown enough promise to maintain future optimism.

 Kerry's reported thoughts filtered through. She was satisfied; the
horse would have learnt a lot both physically and mentally in
terms of the horserace experience. The jockey though didn't seem
to be in the good books. There were mutterings about the ride and
some questioned whether he hadn't ridden to instructions.

I would imagine this is very hard to do in a bumper where lots of
very keen horses are pulling and literally raring to go. He
certainly hadn't taken too much out of the horse once passed and
surely this would be a good thing in terms of the future.
So there would be no prize money and my modest each way
wager was not destined to raise any returns but there was some
promise in this starting run.

My own view was this might be a long-term prospect for the Lees
or Foxtrot; I of course was more interested in the short term. We
made our way on foot from the course, through the impressive
town centre of Warwick; it had been a great day out at a very
pleasant course.

Needless to say all the train connections worked and we were back in a Manchester hostelry in two hours, able to assess what the day had told us.

**Monday 16ᵗʰ January**
The Racing Post's pithy summary for DTS; 'edged right…weakened from four furlongs out', was not enough to dampen enthusiasm for the horses Warwick performance. There was an upbeat feel to correspondence. Kerry reported that the horse had eaten up well, was happy and would have a relaxing week cantering through the local woods. They would then step it up and there were some thoughts about going racing again in around three weeks.

This sounded good to me and I made a note of the three possible bumper races mentioned. Exeter would certainly stretch my devotion as it was a long way to go, but Towcester and Chepstow all seemed within my compass. I was still hoping and assuming that the horse would appear at its local tracks of Ludlow or Hereford, but there had been no mention of this. It would seem that although they might be appropriately located courses they don't always have the races that Kerry Lee is looking at.

**Wednesday 25ᵗʰ January**
DTS is apparently schooling really well, Kerry is reported to be delighted and excited with his jumping ability. All three-bumper engagements are still under consideration.
News has also filtered through regarding Herefordshire. 'Our' old horse is still on box rest but after consideration it has been decided to curtail his nascent chasing career and he will return to pointing next winter. Age apparently, wasn't on his side.

**Friday 27ᵗʰ January**
Just a couple of days after this news we are told that Kerry will be putting a stable visit together on March 25ᵗʰ for our 'new' horse.

This seems a long time away, but a quick check of the diary tells me it's a free football weekend and that Hereford has a race meeting on the same weekend, so I'm happy with that. I email Dan with my acceptance.

# CHAPTER 6
# FEBRUARY

**Tuesday 7th February**
DTS receives an entry for both Exeter and Towcester. The Exeter race on Sunday the twelfth of February has attracted thirty-nine entries; Kerry thinks he will get into this race, if she decides to run him. I much prefer the other option at Towcester, apparently Kerry will decide when she has compared likely runners.
I have a quick look at the BHA list of entries at Exeter and even to my untrained eye they look a very strong bunch. Quite a few of them had runs under their belt and some had already chalked up a win, indeed there is a McManus horse that has run twice and won twice.

I hope the entries put Kerry off the Exeter run.

**Wednesday 8th February**
DTS will not run at Exeter, it's judged to be an extremely competitive race.

 Good, I'm quite pleased about that outcome; it would be a long way to go for three minutes action. More pertinently, Towcester now becomes a real possibility. I go to check the train timetables, and good news there looks to be a fast Virgin train direct from Manchester to Milton Keynes with a bus service to Towcester. I keep my fingers crossed that this time the entries will be more manageable, although I have a feeling we might race regardless.

**Friday 10th February**
DTS has as expected been entered to race at Towcester next Wednesday. My Racing Post site shows me the twenty-six entries and this time they don't seem quite so threatening. Point of Principle, DTS's conqueror at Warwick was on the list, but quite a

few hadn't run before. I'm very confident now that Kerry will want to run him.

An email later in the day confirms this but it contains a worrying caveat. Apparently DTS is not guaranteed a run because he may be balloted out of the race, as there are too many horses! There is a set criterion for this situation and Dan was very informative. The first is that there is a safety limit for the number of horses allowed to run. In this particular race it was sixteen. Secondly over the whole meeting, each horse raced must have it's own box on race day and Towcester can only stable eighty-five horses. Therefore the number of horses declared for the other five races will determine the final number in the last race, that figure could fall to twelve. Apparently of the twenty-six horses entered, DTS is the fifth horse to be balloted out of the race, if the number declared goes above the permitted field size. In other words if the field size was sixteen, DTS would need five horses to drop out.

I am somewhat perplexed by this and once again I'm sweating on a declaration. My old racing pal Gordon is a member at Towcester and I make a loose arrangement to meet up with him on the day, assuming DTS gets into the race. When I mention the possible dilemma he cheers me up by telling me lots usually drop out between entry and declaration stage. I am less certain.

## Tuesday 14th February
It's my daughter's birthday, and she brings us the requisite luck because despite my concerns only twelve horses are declared and of course DTS is amongst them.

Jamie Moore is apparently serving a ban, but I'm impressed to hear that Sam Twiston-Davies has been booked to ride. Kerry sounds upbeat, she's been delighted with the horse since Warwick but sounds the usual cautionary note by saying the horse will be better when he's jumping, and better over the longer distance.

Well that sounds a long way off; I'm just pleased to see him on the racecourse. His race will be the last one on the card at four forty, a flat race of one mile seven furlongs. Kerry hopes we will see an improvement from Warwick and is looking forward to tomorrow. Amen to that.

*　　*　　*

## RACEDAY – DESTINED TO SHINE AT TOWCESTER, WEDNESDAY, 15, FEBRUARY
## THE RACECOURSE

Communication modes were once again totally efficient, as the train raced from Manchester to Milton Keynes. There was even plenty of room allowing me to peruse the runners in that mornings Racing Post. DTS was to face a select but competitive field featuring the usual big stable hopefuls and some bumper experienced horses.

My old racing partner Les was once more in attendance due to Foxtrot's good offices and we met at Milton Keynes. Hopefully it was not a sign of things to come as Les got us on the local bus to Towcester that seemed to take almost as long as my train journey from Manchester! Once ensconced in the Plough we were able to grab a couple of pints of good quality beer before making our way up the road to the racecourse, about a mile outside the town.

The racecourse is located adjacent to the county estate of Lord Hesketh (of motor car racing fame), and there is a large brick wall that runs along the perimeter of the course that eventually leads us to the remarkable stone gateway that brings you through and onto Towcester racecourse.

Towcester, is unique in terms of British racecourses, in that it doesn't charge an entrance fee, the racing is free. Gordon (who we met at the course) explained that this has been the case for a while, although I wasn't quite sure how it is funded apart from the fact that all the food vendors are paying their fees.

The Course Inspector had generally written nice things about Towcester sixteen years before summarising it thus; ' a country estate racecourse with a splendid stone gateway and natural panorama of middle England'. As we wandered down from the gate towards the main stand it quickly became apparent that the panorama had changed radically.

A greyhound-racing track has been constructed and placed directly in front of the main grandstand. While this no doubt is helpful to spectators of the dogs, it has had the effect of wiping out a good portion of the panoramic view referred to by Mr Lee. Indeed once the horses have raced past you and head out into the country they disappear from view and you have to train the binoculars on the large TV screen. Gordon told me that before the dog track appeared three years ago, one had spectacular views of the rolling Northamptonshire countryside and villages as the horses raced away in the distance, now punters struggle to see any more than half the course. Sacrilege really, I don't know what the inspector would make of it, but I'm pretty sure it would lead to a minus mark.

Towcester is certainly a hilly, challenging course, the oft-repeated joke that it is uphill all the way around, seems distinctly possible. It's clearly a stiff course to ride, riding a waiting race could be particularly challenging. Timeforms summary seemed apt: 'right handed with an extremely stiff final mile uphill', adding humorously, 'and not unknown for horses to falter on catching sight of the stable entrance on the run in on the racetrack'. Whether DTS would need such a refuge only time would tell. The weather was visibly changing, the morning's sunshine was giving way to heavy cloud and there was rain in the air as we located the owners and trainers facilities.

These were located in a large tent behind the parade ring. Usually at arriving at a racecourse one has to check in with reception staff at the main office, but that was not the case at this course. The friendly gate keeper to the tent seemed to be the one man reception committee as on enquiry he motioned with his thumb where the owners facilities were and in the same motion delivered a couple of owners badges for the afternoon.

The owners and trainers tent was busy but not unpleasant and we were able to grab a couple of free chairs and plenty of the complimentary tea and biscuits. However the complimentary race card was not to be seen, despite Les's exhaustive search of the premises. It seemed to me that the one man who might be able to solve this conundrum, was located by the gate, and sure enough he once more dipped into those large pockets and proffered a couple of racecards.

A quick look through the good quality programme told me that this was where the quality stopped, the six races were characterised by a lot of low BHA ratings and some very short priced favourites. Out of the corner of my eye I noticed the ex football Manager Harry Rednapp was in attendance. He was sat fiddling with his phone, maybe fixing up a potential transfer, one could imagine that might be a hard habit for him to lose, even when no longer a manager (he actually returned to management later in the season, for a brief sojourn as boss of Birmingham City). Curious, I quickly thumbed through the programme to see which horse belonged to him, it was called Drumlee City, and needless to say, it was in the DTS race!

*       *       *

PRERACE
The pleasant early morning weather had definitely disappeared and as the afternoon progressed the rain intensified. Now it seemed virtually everybody was in the owners and trainers tent

avoiding the constant downpour. I wasn't having a good day punting wise, not having a sniff of a winner until the race before the bumper, a race which exemplified the difficulties of racing at Towcester. After a gruelling three-mile chase through increasingly heavy ground some exhausted horses struggled up the demanding finish with the lead constantly changing hands. Suddenly my fancy Leith Hill Legasi hit the front with just yards left to run and the race at his mercy, only to be beaten in the final strides.

Mild disappointment was put to one side as we marched down to the pre parade ring to see how DTS was dealing with the preliminaries.

However, there was no sign of him as a couple of other horses paraded in front of us. Suddenly the calm was broken as one horse, Carrie On Dubai broke free from his handlers and briefly threatened to run amok until he was caught and restrained. The horses had all moved through to the parade ring proper before DTS suddenly appeared, looking reasonably calm as he did a circuit of the parade ring. Despite the rainfall the DTS 'partners', were here in strength, Dan had once more worked the oracle. As the rain was not relenting, the usual pleasantries were kept to a minimum as Richard Lee appeared, as at Ffos Las he was here in Kerry's stead.

At this point our jockey for the afternoon, Sam Twiston-Davies appeared, acknowledging the group and outlining his plans for the ride. Sam has become something of a pin up boy for modern jump racing, being clean cut, enthusiastic and articulate. Being the champion trainer Paul Nichols, retained rider, he is obviously pretty good at his chosen profession. We were lucky to have him today and that together with the rainfall (Kerry Lee's horses tend to do well in soft conditions) made me a little more upbeat regarding our chances.

Sam was conscious of the horse's immaturity, and told us he would look for some cover in the early part of the race and then try to get the horse involved at the finish. With that he quickly mounted and disappeared out of the parade ring, as we scurried for cover.

As we dispersed I suddenly remembered I hadn't placed my bet and I quickly monitored the tote and bookmaker prices. The upbeat feeling was quickly dissipated, as it was obvious that DTS was friendless and drifting in the market. Sometimes you can get better value on the tote, but today the bookies were beating their 16-1 price, and I placed £5 each way at 20-1. If I had waited another minute or so I would have seen it drift out to 25-1. All the money was on Astrapaios, Storm Nelson and Cadeym, virtually joint favourites at 3-1. Betting is by definition unpredictable, and our connections hadn't told us much, other than they hoped DTS would run better than at Warwick. Betting on a bumper is even more unpredictable as many of the horses either had not run before or their experience is somewhat limited. Maybe there was a little value to be had in my small bet that was clearly dictated by loyalty to 'my' horse. The ready reckoners that can be used to translate odds into percentage chances tell us that a horse running at odds of 25-1 has a three percent chance of wining and a ninety seven percent chance of not wining. Somewhat prohibitive perhaps, but I had not come all this way, not to back Destined.

With the bet placed, we made our way upstairs in the main stand, an area limited to the 'corporates 'with their private boxes and the owners involved in that particular race. We were led into a spacious room with a balcony adjacent to the finishing line. With the binoculars I could see DTS in the far distance lining up for his second competitive race.

*       *       *

## THE RACE-NATIONAL HUNT FLAT RACE (CLASS 6), 1MILE 7 FURLONGS

The race started in farcical circumstances. The fancied Nigel Twiston-Davies horse Corzeam dug in his heels and refused to start, as the other horses set off. As if that wasn't enough of a drama, Carrie on Dubai, who had misbehaved in the pre parade ring, started to do an imitation of a 'bucking bronco' and after careering sideways at the starting point, jettisoned its unfortunate jockey.

DTS perhaps distracted by the shenanigans behind him started a little skittishly, veering slightly to his right, Sam clearly had his hands full steering him onto a straight course. The horse was pulling hard and Sam struggling to reign in the horses enthusiasm, allowed the horse to power forward and take the lead. So much, for the pre race plan!

Once in front, DTS bowled merrily along and passed us for the first time adjacent with the finishing post. The rest of the field bunched together closely behind the early leader. He certainly looked full of running as he skated over the drenched surface, and from our exalted position high up on the owner's balcony we could clearly see DTS take the field into the country. Les was impressed, 'he's going well' he ventured; I thought a quieter countenance was a wise precaution. He had started in a similar vein at Warwick and of course there most of the field eventually passed him.

Non-the less, he certainly looked comfortable as he passed the half way stage, with the rest of the field just beginning to look a little strung out. As they moved back towards the demanding home straight it certainly looked as if 'our' horse's strong pace had done for some of the field, as they were patently struggling and off the bridle. At the bottom of the hill, there looked to be a group of about five horses that were in with a chance, but incredibly DTS looked to be going best and clearly now had a serious chance.

The big question now was how would DTS cope with the demanding uphill finish, given his exuberant front running tactics and the fact four other horses were grouped behind him. I needn't have worried, as now at this crucial juncture DTS seemed to start going away from the field, now the quieter countenance was jettisoned, as I began to shout Sam home. Harry Rednapp's Drumlee City tried to go with him, but as they moved over the final two hundred yards, DTS went away to win the race comfortably, by four lengths.

*    *    *

**POSTRACE**
Well this was truly the romance of horse racing; DTS our 'replacement' horse on only his second run ever, had totally surprised us all and won the race at 25-1!
He hadn't seen another horse, as they say, winning the race in the most thrilling fashion.

Almost stunned into silence I made my way down to the winner's enclosure, not something I had envisaged at any point in the afternoon. Despite the increasingly wet and gloomy environment, there were a jubilant group of 'partners', cheering and taking photographs of the returning horse and jockey. Whilst ready to join in with the celebrations, I was conscious this was the last race of the day and I wanted to collect my winnings before the bookies disappeared. Luckily Gordon was on hand and kindly went to collect my winnings, while I returned to the backslapping and congratulations.

Sam now returned on top of DTS, there was hardly a mark on him, in contrast to the other mud-splattered jockeys. Incredibly, he started to almost apologise about the change in tactics that had been forced by the antics at the start of the race. He gave an articulate debrief, where he emphasised how well DTS had travelled and that the horse had stayed really well up that challenging hill finish.

It's obviously pleasant for a jockey when he returns to an appreciative audience (often, particularly in the last race, there may be nobody there) and he said all the right things in terms of the horse's potential. "Yes" he thought, he could be a good one with the 'potential' to go onto good things. Richard, in his usual impassive way, claimed he would be a good jumper. Suddenly it seemed the World was our oyster.

With the light now fading fast, the partners lined up for the official photographs. Luckily, I had been in this position before a couple of times over the last few years, but this was certainly the sweetest in the sense that it was totally unexpected.

I also knew what would follow and indeed we were invited back up to the room were we had witnessed the race to meet the course representative and enjoy watching the race again with a glass of bubbly. Now we were all full of DTS's moment of glory, 'never saw another horse' claimed one partner, 'he was going away at the finish' said another. Despite the 'bit of fun' school and 'just having a horse taking part is the main thing' philosophy, nothing beats having a winning horse. Given the early season frustrations and demise of the unfortunate Herefordshire and the patience needed to reach this point, this was understandably a special moment.

Of course now I had a bigger share in this horse than previously, so would collect a bigger slice of the winnings, once deductions had occurred. Together with my winning punt, this had turned into a profitable day. The actual winning sum recorded in the Racing Post was £1949. A paltry sum given the days of training put into the horse and owners investment and reflects badly on British horse racing. Clearly it is a profitable industry, but I can assure you dear reader that the profits made are not being returned to owners, trainers or jockeys who will get a small slice of such a sum.

Still such contentious issues are for another day, and a winner is a winner, and for the 'I really gotta horse' project of mine this was a swift and surprising return given our early season frustrations. These were interesting thoughts as I returned to Manchester, seemingly on cloud nine given the DTS heroics. On my return that night, my inbox contained an email from the ever efficient, Dan that confirmed it wasn't an illusion, DTS had won at Towcester. There was even a link that enabled, both myself, and Sue, to watch the race all over again. Yes, Towcester on February fifteenth, proved to be quite a day.

## THURSDAY 16th FEBRUARY
Well I suppose I shouldn't be to blasé about yesterdays win. It was only a few weeks ago that the papers had been full of the owner from Sussex, who had waited twenty-seven years and two hundred and fifty races to record his first winner. This was the third time I had been in the winner's enclosure in the last three years so I should consider myself to be the lucky one.

The news this morning from the stable is that DTS has 'eaten up', a term used to relay back to owners the good health of the horse after yesterdays exertions. The horse was not surprisingly having an easy time with a day off in a field. The relationship between trainer and syndicate partners, has now probably changed, two days ago we had a green novice with one run, today we have a winner. Mr Lee owns the horse, but of course the partners have paid all the training fees for this years activities. It will be interesting to see how this pans out from here.

## SUNDAY 19th FEBRUARY
Foxtrot's weekly bulletin comes through and it would seem DTS has kick-started the club into three winners in five days.
Given that they are dealing at the value end of the market, their

statistics over the past year are quite phenomenal. Dan is quick to point out that Foxtrot's 31% win rate is some 13% higher than the esteemed Mr McManus, music to my ears!

**WEDNESDAY 22nd FEBRUARY**
It looks like we may get some hurdling action out of DTS before the lease and season comes to a close. Today an email arrives with a picture of DTS jumping very stylishly over a hurdle. Apparently DTS has schooled well over the hurdles and could be a natural over the obstacles. This is exciting news, and if we manage to get to a hurdles race this will be a nice compensation for the chaser that we so unfortunately lost to injury. However, Kerry stresses the horse's immaturity and says that she wants more time before she decides on future race plans.

**FRIDAY 24th FEBRUARY**
The promised DVD of DTS's Towcester victory arrived today. Well packaged, with a pleasant covering letter from Dan, that told us to enjoy the rerun of the race, and the 'brilliant performance of our five year old'.

 From what I can gather, if your horse wins a race, the racecourse, send the owners a DVD of the race. Dan has done really well to make copies so that all of us get the bona fide owners copy. This is another feature of how the ownership lark has improved for the small owner. I seem to remember, Stan Hey waiting six months for some sort of video of one of his horses, there is no doubt communications have improved significantly since then.

# CHAPTER 7
# MARCH 2017

**THURSDAY 2nd MARCH**

March is the most important month of the year for the National Hunt race fan because that is when the Cheltenham festival occurs. A festival of all the top class National Hunt horses was hardly likely to feature DTS, but I did wonder if 'our' horse might be running elsewhere that week. I get my tickets well in advance for 'Chelts' and I would have a bit of a dilemma on my hands if DTS were entered to race elsewhere during the festival. The three-week gap from his last race until the festival, to my mind, made an entry, quite feasible.

However this morning's news from the trainer maybe made this scenario less likely. Apparently DTS had lost a little 'condition', which I believe means that he is not in tip top physical shape. Kerry wants to deal with this over the next week or so, before committing to a specific race plan. It would seem that she is still somewhat undecided whether his next race will be a hurdle race or another bumper. Of course if he ran in another bumper, he will have to carry extra weight as a penalty for his Towcester success, so that may be a factor in her decision. It is mentioned somewhat tentatively, that he may be entered for a hurdle race at Southwell on March 20th, or if it's to be a bumper it could be Carlisle on the fifth of April. That seems a long time off to me, and although Carlisle is a particular favourite of mine, I think I would prefer the Southwell fixture.

As always, the trainer will have the final say.

**SUNDAY 11th MARCH**

The week before Cheltenham proved to be a quiet one in terms of news and the silence seems to indicate that nothing is imminent, although I assume Southwell on the twentieth is still the plan. Foxtrot, have a runner at the Cheltenham festival, which is quite an achievement.

## WEDNESDAY 15th MARCH

I have a moderately good day at the festival and this is enhanced by the news that DTS is indeed entered for Southwell. Although of course this is not a declaration, I am pleased, I quite fancy the Nottingham course; it's not far from my home, a consideration when I joined the partnership last year. The other positive is if declared, this will be a hurdle race, which would be a good result given where we were starting from at the end of December.

Apparently there are a lot of entries for the race, thirty-two in all. It's a possibility that if a lot of those are declared, the race could be split into two. At this stage, the news from the trainer is she is keen to run him, with the usual caveats.

I was emboldened enough to check out Southwell's location and the available train connections. It looks good, I can be there on the train in a couple of hours, and I'll keep everything crossed.

## SATURDAY 16th MARCH

Cheltenham week is over and completed enjoyably. A bit of my old lucky punting ways returned on the last day, as I managed to spot a Gordon Elliott horse in the morning at 33-1, it later won with half of Ireland on it, at 12-1.

I could now concentrate on DTS. I had heard nothing to the contrary and although declarations had still not been announced, I thought I better check out Mr J and see if he fancied Monday's imminent trip. He was very much up for it, so we sorted out the potential train times and I told him I would ring him back on Sunday with all the details. That done, and almost as an afterthought I went to check my morning emails.

'Disappointed Dunskies'! To para phrase Johnny Boy in Martin Scorsese's film, Mean Streets. There waiting in the inbox was the email titled, 'Destined To Shine will not run at Southwell on Monday'. This was very disappointing news. Kerry apparently had not been totally happy with yesterday's schooling and on that basis had decided not to run. There still appears to be some uncertainty as to whether this next engagement will be over hurdles or another bumper.

Outside of the immediate frustration of another potential race-day disappearing paranoia now sets in. It is now over a month since the Towcester race and the positive reports indicated the horse was doing well; it is therefore somewhat puzzling to not find him on a racecourse. I can understand large time gaps with a big chaser who probably needs time to get over his races, but DTS has just bowled around a couple of flat races in the three months we've had him. Despite all the upbeat reports regarding his schooling, could there be a problem with his hurdling? Obviously the horse is young and learning the game, but this lease is a limited one and there are only six weeks left of the contract. To make matters worse, the Carlisle bumper that I quite fancy is not mentioned in the latest communication, setting up dark thoughts in my mind about the next race being at Exeter!

I relay the unfortunate news to Mr J, my history teaching, colleague at a modern College of some twenty years plus. It doesn't look as though I will be visiting Southwell after all. The course inspector had referred to the course as;' a diverting spot for Historians, a decent base for forest ramblers and the ideal self indulgence for inveterate gamblers'. Oh well, for that Historian, it was not to be.

## SUNDAY 19th MARCH
The Foxtrot newsletter confirms DTS's non-appearance, and delivers the standard line, that we must be guided by the trainer. This brings to mind Kate Fox, and her book. 'The Racing Tribe'. In

the book she accords the trainer with a witch doctor status, in which their decisions are sacrosanct.

The stable visit is next Saturday; it will be interesting to gauge the mood and opinion of some of the partners.

## FRIDAY 24th MARCH

Arrive in Hereford for a three-day break with Sue. I've thoughtfully nominated this as a break for our wedding anniversary! Hereford is a beautiful City with much in the way of culture and beautiful walking territory, I am sure this will satisfy my other half. We are staying at the Green Dragon, perfectly located in the centre of the City, close to the splendid Cathedral.

I think the hotel has seen better days, but it pervades a kind of old World charm and is certainly convenient for tomorrow's drive to the stables at Byton.

It was while sampling what Hereford's famous Barrels pub had to offer that I received a late email from Dan. It contained the news that DTS's owner Richard had decided to sell the horse, and we had some kind of first option at what seemed to be an astronomical price. Although I wasn't likely to change my own plan of just having this one season with the horse, this was clearly big news for the syndicate. In the future this would not be a lease, but an opportunity for the syndicate to buy the horse outright. Clearly if the syndicate thought this was a good idea, then they would have complete ownership of the horse, but would have to pool their resources to buy the horse and then pay the fees to train the animal. Although purely a technical issue to me, I could see the advantages of controlling the destiny (no pun intended) of the horse, but I could also see the much greater costs involved. What also became apparent, was that there was little advantage in the Lees running this horse from this date, as they would be taking a risk that the horse's next run would be less impressive and this would damage the price they would be looking to achieve at market. In some respects this was quite a dilemma for them and I began to wonder about the Southwell non-appearance. However, it was the 'partners' that had paid all the training fees thus far, and there was still some six weeks left on the agreed lease. Clearly this intensified the Lees dilemma.

This news certainly makes for an interesting backdrop to tomorrows stable visit. From my own point of view, I can see both sides, but clearly I paid in for this season and I expect more runs before the end of the lease. DTS is clearly a very promising athletic horse and I'm sure Kerry is right when she claims he will make a good chaser. However, there is a significant time spell between now and then and a lot of things can go wrong, as we saw with the unfortunate Herefordshire. DTS is right at the start of his career and although we were delighted with his bumper win, I am reminded that Chilly Miss in *"Four Hooves and a Prayer"*, actually won two bumpers and eventually turned out to be a game if moderate performer.

We will see what tomorrow brings.

## SATURDAY 26th MARCH

We are greeted by brilliant March sunshine as we made our way up onto the gallops at Byton. This really is quite stunning country and the 'partners' are here in strength. DTS along with three other horses gallop up the steep hill towards the 'partners', who are situated at the top of the hill. The horse looks in excellent condition and today we are to be given the extra treat of seeing him school over hurdles. This to my untrained eye he seems to achieve with aplomb, two or three times doing a stint of jumping the three hurdles set out in front of him.

Kerry, who has arrived with Richard, now calls us together, to give a debrief on his progress. She emphasises that he is still a baby that is learning the ropes, but she clearly thinks a lot of his ability and believes he is going to make up to be a top class horse. She doesn't dodge the issue of ownership and reiterates that she wants the syndicate to stay in the yard, but she reminds us, that she's in a business.

I canvass opinion from some of the partners that I have got to know over the last six months, and if they are anything to go by, I don't think Kerry is going to get the deal she is after.
We drive from the gallops to the Lees farm, where they have kindly put some food on, which is very welcome. Kerry circulates showing us pictures of her horse Top Gamble (who is one of her best chasers) and telling us that he reminds her of DTS at the same age. There is no doubt that Kerry is genuinely enthusiastic about DTS and sees him as a chaser in the making.

Surprisingly nobody appears to be wandering down to the stables to see 'our' horse, so together with Sue I meander down the cobbled path to check how he is after his morning exertions. The stable girls are mucking out, but there at the end stable, DTS is to be found munching through his feed. He's a friendly horse, but we have been warned not to touch the horses, so I stand a respectful distance for the photographs.

It's been an interesting morning. Stable visits are very much part of the 'ownership' experience and today's one in brilliant sunshine has made up for the lack of racing in March. The fact that we have managed two visits in the lease is a major positive.

### SUNDAY 26th MARCH
We completed our pleasant three-day visit to Hereford with a trip to its racecourse. I had expected that we would have come here before in an official capacity with H, but it was not to be.
The course has struggled in the recent past, faced closure and had only reopened this season. I was most impressed with the course, which was packed on this day, the crowd basking in the sunshine. On the journey back I gave some thought to the ongoing 'ownership' issue. I had the feeling that Foxtrot were not in any rush to take up any offer at the prices mentioned, but I was

pleased to see that nights email emphasised the 'partners' wanted to enjoy the time left in the existing lease. More to the point, Carlisle was back on the agenda, and the news seemed fairly definite, DTS would run early next month.

## FRIDAY 31st MARCH

Some positive news at the end of a blank month of racing, DTS is indeed entered for Carlisle next Wednesday. Of course this doesn't mean he will be declared, but I'm optimistic. The partners I spoke to on the stable visit seemed to think Carlisle was unlikely and Ffos Las more of an option. If he does run at Carlisle it will be interesting to see how many of the 'partners' show up. There are nineteen entries and Kerry is apparently keen for him to run as long as the going stays soft. We have had a little bit of wet weather recently and I know that Carlisle is more likely to remain soft so I am encouraged. Equally the news that Kerry is already talking about booking her usual jockey Jamie Moore for the ride further increases my optimism that we might have a race at Carlisle. However, I'm not getting carried away, let's face it, we have had entries before.

I send Dan an email in response to his summary about the issue of the future ownership of DTS. I have kept a low profile in terms of communications, preferring to keep a watching brief, but this issue has become so pertinent, I decide to send a short note. Rather than involving myself in the pros and cons of the individual ownership issue, I stress that the important thing is to obtain some more racing in this particular lease. Dan seems to agree with this, saying; lets see what next week brings.

# CHAPTER 8
# APRIL 2017

**Sunday 2ⁿᵈ April**

The month is starting on a positive note. Although the short wet spell is finished and the weather forecast for the week is dry, the going at Carlisle is still reported as 'soft'. The weekly newsletter reiterates that DTS is likely to run at Carlisle.
I remain cautiously optimistic.

**Tuesday 4ᵗʰ April**

According to the Racing Post site, the going at Carlisle has changed to, 'good to soft'. I needn't worry though because an hour later the good news comes through that DTS has been declared to run at Carlisle. I check the RP again, and Destined is at the top of a list of twelve horses that will contest the two mile one furlong bumper. This field looks manageable, with only three others having run before. That said, one of them Ouro Branco, has already won a bumper at Carlisle and there are some expensive recruits amongst the debutants.

I immediately put in for a couple of badges, Dan responds positively, but tells me, he can't make tomorrow. It will be interesting to see how many of the 'partners' are going to travel 'up north'.

I spend the night before assessing the race. Having now won a race, DTS is respected and amongst the fancied runners. However, because of that win, DTS is penalised and has to carry more weight than any other horse in the race, clearly this will be a hindrance to his chances of winning. Ouro Branco, has also won, but because he is a year younger, he carries less weight than our hero.

The well-informed At the Races site writes up our chances; 'Debut run wasn't devoid of promise and he emphatically built on that when landing a twelve runner contest in the mud at Towcester in February. Well ridden that day, but still a player under a penalty'. Luckime, is a debutant that will be fancied, as he is a Trevor Hemmings horse, and therefore costly, trained by Venetia Williams. Similarly the Lucinda Russell horse, Dr Hooves, cost one hundred and thirty thousand Euros, so is bound to attract support. There are plenty of horses though, that have a modest background and I think we have cautious grounds for optimism. Timeform, the bible of horse race ratings and data, again gave cause for optimism. Although it plumped for Ouro Bravo (bound to be a short priced favourite) to win the race, it thought DTS could 'remain competitive' and it predicted a second place finish.

Secretly, I'd be happy with that, although it clearly had chances of going one better. The weight was probably going to be a critical factor and it might come down to how he could cope with the extra burden, on going that although partly soft may not be his perfect ground. I was just delighted to be going to Carlisle tomorrow, it would definitely make up for the non-appearance at Southwell. It would enable us to visit what has become something of a local course to us, in addition to which we could take a two-day break in the Lake District. It's when things like this come together, that the 'I really gotta a horse' project can really be judged a success.

*     *     *

**RACEDAY – DESTINED TO SHINE AT CARLISLE, WEDNESDAY, 5th APRIL**
**THE RACECOURSE**
Of course I had been to Carlisle before as an owner, with the whole hearted if limited jumper Brunello (**"Four Hooves and a Prayer"**) in May of 2015. The course, located in the pleasant

countryside of Blackwell village, just outside Carlisle City centre, remains amongst my favourites. I'm certainly familiar now with the owner's facilities, which are impressive. There will not be any obstacles to jump today, but the course is a relatively tight right-handed one and the uphill finish should remind DTS of Towcester.

With our race the last one on the card, this allowed myself, and Sue plentiful time to enjoy the excellent complimentary sausage and mash in the owners building.

It was busy in the owners and trainers facility, the weather had turned a touch colder and it seemed that most 'connections' had headed to this building for shelter from the wind.

On the way to Carlisle, I had received the not altogether surprising news that I could expect just one other owner in attendance this afternoon. It would seem that for one reason or another, the 'partners' had decided to give Carlisle a wide berth. Well, as Dan emailed, more champagne for me! By default it would seem that I was ending up with a scenario that such small horse owners can only dream about. In past racing clubs I had been involved in, there could have been thousands of members, a lucky draw for a paddock place and if successful, one face amongst many encircling trainer and jockey. Now I had the prospect, that I would be one of only two 'owners' present, with exclusive access to trainer and jockey. As things transpired, it actually got better than this.

*     *     *

**PRERACE**
With our race last on the card, we had time to enjoy some relatively competitive low-grade races; I even managed to find a reasonably priced winner of the feature race.
When the time came for the last race we made our way down

towards the parade ring, where I spotted Richard standing in glorious isolation.

There was no sign of any other 'partner', and I subsequently found out that on this day at Carlisle I would be the only 'owner' present. The parade ring still had a group with Lucinda Russell present; they were celebrating having just won the previous race. In just three days time, she would be celebrating once more, as her horse One for Arthur, was destined to win the Grand National.

I made my way over to Richard, introducing myself, and my wife. Richard was charm personified. Greeting us warmly, he too thought there was supposed to be another owner present, but it soon became apparent that today I was to have his undivided attention. This was quite a unique situation made even more interesting by the fact it was such a crucial race for the future of DTS. Firstly, it was going to be a test to see if he could live up to his sterling achievement at Towcester and secondly it was clearly going to have some kind of impact on the future valuation and sale of the horse.

I immediately engaged Richard on the state of health of our steed. Richard confirmed he was in top class condition, had been working well at home and that he was looking forward to him running well this afternoon. Richard was definitely a hands on man, on enquiry I found that he had actually driven the horsebox all the way from Byton himself. Indeed of the four runs attended this season, it was noticeable that Kerry had only attended once, Richard had been present at each race. He may have retired the trainer's title to Kerry, but he was clearly still taking an active involvement in affairs.

DTS was now parading in front of us, and Richard possibly alluding to the ownership issue, opined that if he won today he was going to be a 'valuable' horse. Looking down his programme at the list of horses he reiterated that you never quite knew what to expect in bumper races. He highlighted that one of the opposition horses had cost one hundred and thirty thousand Euros, and that there could be 'anything' in the list of runners. We both agreed that the weight factor was going to be important, and Richard kindly explained that the favourite despite its win, was carrying less weight than us because it was a year younger. If he was nervous of the outcome he was hiding it well, remaining courteous and polite.

At this point Jamie Moore, our jockey, joined us. As I was the sole owner present, he shook hands and immediately outlined his thoughts on the upcoming race. Jamie is a friendly outgoing individual and he seemed relatively confident regarding our horse's chances. Although he had not ridden DTS in a competitive race before, he had clearly ridden him on the Lees gallops and appeared to think quite a bit about him. As I was privy to the information from the previous stable visit, I asked were his tactics to hold DTS back and deliver him late in the race. Jamie replied that no he was likely to take it up from the start. Although this seemed to run contrary to the received wisdom, I was quite happy with his response, as I feel Destined could be a strong front runner. Jamie emphasised that DTS was still a 'baby' and as such this afternoon was part of his education and therefore we would see how it went. It all seemed eminently sensible to me and I wished him well as he departed with Richard to mount up.

With the preliminaries over and horse and jockey departing the ring, Richard rejoined us. Jamie it seems is the Lee's stable jockey (their first choice to ride their horses) and he and Richard are clearly an established team. I asked Richard was he his preferred jockey and he confirmed this, adding the fact he valued his straightforward and honest opinion of the horses he rode. This was Jamie's only ride of the day and Richard tells me that he will have driven all the way from his home in Brighton to take up the assignment. Given the modest remuneration on offer, together with the constant threat of injury, one can only take your hat off to these sports-men. In comparison to other sports 'stars', they are a breed apart.

There was a brief interlude as Richard returned to us, given that I had never been in a one to one with a trainer before, I was not sure whether it would be protocol to ask him where he was watching the race from.

The uncertainty didn't last long, as Richard pointed towards the balcony on the old stand, telling us that was where he watched the race from and would we like to join him. This again emphasised the unique nature of today's race-day experience in that clearly I would get an exclusive impression on Richard's view of the race. As we had clambered to the top of the stairs that lead to the balcony, I engaged Richard in some small talk on the two horses he had running in the Grand National. Apparently, he desperately needed rain to soften the going, something that would not transpire.

At this point the chairman of the course James Westoll appeared in our midst, welcoming Richard to Carlisle. They clearly knew each other and entered into some chat revolving around how the racecourse had changed over the years. Richard then kindly introduced myself as the owner, to which Mr Westoll enquired whether I had been to Carlisle before. By that he meant had I owned many horses that had run at Carlisle in the past. This moment was so reminiscent of Lord Cavendish's similar enquiry, when Volcanic won at Cartmel (" *Four Hooves and a Prayer*"), that I again paused and answered that yes I had been to Carlisle many times in the past. True of course, even though only once before as the owner of a horse!

While we were having our chat with the chairman of the course, DTS had decided to jig on the way down to the start and in the process had unshipped Jamie Moore. Once 'loose' he had then careered off to join the other horses at the start, where luckily he was captured. Under normal circumstances this would cause quite some consternation for both trainer and owner. Amazingly, both Richard and myself were oblivious to this late drama and by the time we focused on the starting line, jockey and horse were reunited.

Just before the start of the race, I decided to fully maximise my unique access, by asking him what he expected of 'our' horse. I was expecting a cautious lets see style reply, but Richard surprised me, he was hoping to win the race, he replied.

*    *    *

## THE RACE – NATIONAL HUNT FLAT RACE (CLASS 5), 2 Miles, 1 Furlong

Positioned near the front of the runners, DTS immediately moved into the lead as the yellow flag signalled the start of the race. Destined seemed keen and was pulling slightly, but Jamie soon settled him and he quickly moved into a three furlong lead over the others. Jamie's tactics were exactly as he outlined to me before the race and Destined seemed full of running and comfortable in the lead. Many of the favoured horses were in the pack immediately behind 'our' horse as the race reached the halfway stage.

I trained my binoculars on Destined, whereas Richard viewed the large screen, saying nothing as the race took shape. As they reached the back straight with three quarter of a mile left to run, DTS was still controlling events, with a couple of lengths lead and to my eye, going really well. At the bottom of the hill, the front four were well clear of the field and although DTS maintained his lead, the two-pre race favourites Ouro Branco and Luckime were gaining ground and primed to make their challenge. Going up the hill, Jamie moved DTS to the stand side, but the other two horses along with Court Affairs were almost in a line now. Despite the extra weight, galvanised by Jamie, Destined bravely fought off the challenge of the favourites, going away from the soon beaten Ouro Branco and repelling Luckime. Unfortunately, it was the outsider, Court Affairs that went past 'our' boy over the final furlong to win the race. That final effort had taken it out of DTS and in the final yards he was passed by Luckime, to finish the race in third place.

It had been an exciting spectacle, I thought DTS had run a pretty good race and at one stage looked like he might stay on and win first prize. (The winner won £1734, whereas a measly £287 was due for coming third). This money wasn't going to go far amongst the 'partners', in addition to which I had lost my £20 bet as I'd boldly gone for a straight win. After a respectful minute, I asked Richard what he thought of the outcome, to which there was no reply. Undeterred I asked again, as Richard was scribbling the winning distances between the horses onto his programme, we'll see what Jamie says, he eventually replied.

\*        \*        \*

## POSTRACE
While I greeted the horse on his return to the parade ring, Richard and Jamie had a brief confab. Shortly after which, Jamie walked around the horse to address myself. He was pleased with the run and definite in his opinion that the only reason we didn't win the race, was the extra weight he had to carry. The weight stopped him in the final furlong, he said. I enquired about the going and whether this was a mitigating factor, with it not being the ideal. However, Jamie thought the going was Ok and overall it hadn't been a factor. Richard had joined us by now as we looked on as DTS gulped the water down, following his exertions. He's still a baby, they both agreed, he's learning, this race will further his education, was the consensus.

Richard who had listened quietly, possibly mindful of what the run may or may not have done to the horses valuation, now returned to a favourite theme. That the horse was a 'good'un', who would make up into a good jumper, in future seasons. Jamie concurred; yes he will be a good one for next season, 'depending on what you guys want to do'. This reference to the ongoing debate on the future ownership of the horse, showed how pertinent the issue was. I sidestepped that issue and asked him how good the horse could be next year.

Jockeys no doubt have an innate awareness of how good a horse can be; probably based on the hundreds of horses they have ridden in the past. In line with the frank and revealing insights I had gained all afternoon, Jamie shot back, that the horse could be a 125 – 130 rated horse. I'd learnt enough about horses over the last four years of 'ownership' to be able to interpret his answer. In July of 2016, just before I joined this syndicate, there were 3,573 horses with an official BHA hurdle rating. The lowest figure recorded was 50, the highest 174 and the median average at that time was 107.

DTS was due to go hurdling next season, so if Jamie's figure proved correct than he would prove to be well above average, although clearly no World-beater. It was therefore a reasonable endorsement, DTS could turn out to be a good horse able to compete in the better grade races. Of course the Lees were more renowned for their chasers, and given this horses build and athleticism, they thought or certainly hoped that he would in fact turn out to be an even higher rated chaser.

With the parade ring clearing I shook hands with Jamie and wished him the best of luck in the upcoming Grand National. Richard had asked the groom to take DTS away and as he left the parade ring, I thought in all probability this would be the last time he might race for 'us', either this season or indeed in the future. Richard and Jamie had inferred as much, although with three weeks left on the lease, we would no doubt get the usual line on potential entries.

Richard, who had been the perfect host for the afternoon, bade us farewell and we made our way out of the parade ring. We decided against the Chairman's kind offer of a glass of champagne and instead settled for a last cup of tea in the owner's bar.

**Thursday 6th April**
It was a short drive from Carlisle to Ullswater for our overnight stay at the Royal Hotel at Dockrey. This proved to be something of a hidden gem, in the beautiful and less congested north Lakes, indeed we enjoyed a brisk post breakfast climb to the striking, Aira Falls. It was over breakfast, that I noticed an email had arrived from Foxtrot in relation to DTS's race at Carlisle. It told me in case I was in any doubt that DTS had come third at Carlisle and had run a good race. Moreover, it highlighted that the time had come for the 'partners', to decide on whether they wanted to continue with DTS. This effectively meant, did the 'partners' want to bid to own the horse outright, or finish the lease and move on to something else.

Food for thought as we ambled around the edge of Ullswater lake, where sixty two years earlier Donald Campbell had broken the World water speed record, when the iconic Bluebird raced over the surface at 202 miles an hour. DTS was no such speed merchant, but he was a young promising athletic horse, who in time may or may not, make into a good chaser. Going on some of the comments I heard on the recent stable visit, in addition to the asking price, I was fairly certain that the partners would not be taking up the 'offer'. In fact I was very much of a mind that we had actually seen the last run of DTS in 'our' colours.

If that was to be the case, then it made yesterday's exclusive occasion all the more significant. It was days like Wednesday that made my mini project all the more worthwhile, that kind of access, to my mind was the equal of winning a race.

**Sunday 9th April**

DTS has apparently come out of his race well and predictably there was some talk that Kerry wanted to give him a run over hurdles before the season ended.

Whether this is a small incentive to any 'partners' who may want to buy I couldn't say, but surprised me given what I had heard at Carlisle. The next line however, outlined that any such run would be in May, and therefore outside the 'partners' lease.
So it looks as though my impressions at Carlisle were correct. There are no guarantees in horse racing, but four races between the two horses over the lease term is a little disappointing.
Apparently, there is some 'partner' interest in buying DTS and Dan wants further comment from the rest of us. From my own point of view, I had always seen this as a one-year lease and so it wasn't difficult to reject the offer. However, in courtesy to Dan I emailed him the news that I would not be taking up the offer on DTS.

## Monday 10th April
News comes through that there has not been enough 'partner' interest in taking up the ownership offer, so it looks as though Carlisle was to be his final race for us.

I am quite relaxed about this outcome, as I always envisaged it being a one- season arrangement. However, I detect some undertones of frustration from the syndicate's perspective.

## Sunday 16th April
The official news bulletin confirms the news that the 'partnership' has decided against buying DTS, clearly the asking price was not considered to be an attractive option.

## Monday 17th April
Apparently Kerry is still keen to run DTS, but the race will definitely not be before May. I cannot see how this piece of news

is good for anyone really and further underlines the frustrations that have built up over the issue of ownership.

**Wednesday 19<sup>th</sup> April**

News now confirms that DTS will not run again this season! The ground will be too hard and he is off for his holidays.

Kerry it would seem is keen to keep her links with Foxtrot and another horse has been offered for a lease to the partnership. It would seem that in the World of syndicate partnership ownership, life goes on.

# CHAPTER 9
# Postscript

On the first of May 2017 my 'owning' partnership finished, as the syndicated lease on DTS came to an end. So ended my seven-month exercise in 'real' racehorse ownership. As I felt at the time the singular 'ownership' experience I enjoyed at Carlisle proved to be the last time DTS raced. It was time to take stock of the ' I really gotta horse' project that had lasted in one form or another for the previous seven months. Having taught for so many years, it somehow seemed appropriate to reach some conclusions based on my original objectives. It's somewhat ironic that I prided myself on being a student centred teacher and yet here I was reverting to the deadly formula so beloved of the bureaucrats that couldn't teach, but always seemed to end up as Head teachers or College Principals! Yes, they would have said revisit your aims and objectives to assess whether the venture was a success.

**The Horse**
Well of course in the end there were two horses, the unfortunate Herefordshire and his replacement Destined To Shine. In retrospect we were lucky to have a relatively instant replacement, otherwise this project would have reached a somewhat premature conclusion. This potentially, could have been a tricky situation for the syndicate, involving all sorts of recalculation of fees. The contract was a little vague in terms of such eventualities and obviously by this point we had incurred certain training costs, so I for one was happy to still have a horse that could go racing. Non the less, this was definitely a change for the 'partners' to contemplate, we now had a young 'bumper' horse right at the start of its career, not what the 'partners' had signed up for. The initial idea of course was that we were getting a mature 'chaser', specifically trained for the discipline by a trainer who

specialised in such horses. Although we had some action with H, the majority of race time was spent with an unproven horse right at the start of its career. Some 'partners' might have been a little disappointed with this turn of events (although none expressed this to me). From my perspective it allowed continuity and two bites of the cherry, so to speak.

Herefordshire's injury was most unfortunate. However, my recent experiences had taught me that horses were fragile creatures and that when you enter the World of ownership you have be prepared for mishaps. I had known of horses that never actually saw a racecourse, despite the fact that good money had been parted with. As Mr J had often told me, it was very hard to keep horses, particularly big chasers fit throughout a season. Ironically, H's season ending injury was sustained while training and not actually on a racecourse.

So what could one make of the three months and one solitary race that encompassed Herefordshire's racing career? There was definitely a sense of frustration in the early season prolonged wait for acceptable 'going' and a debut run. Aspirations were initially quite high for H, there seemed to be a feeling that H might bring us to some high profile racecourses. In the event Ffos Las was the sum total of such visits. There was an instant readjustment of aspirations following what I thought was a disappointing run. The horse seemed to instantly transfer from the clichéd 'could be anything' label, to lets wait until he gets a lower handicap mark. This original optimism I find endemic with the few race owners I've come across, given his sheltered upbringing, stage of maturity and low mileage, it wasn't an unreasonable assumption for the 'partners' to think they might have a good horse on their hands. However, H's actual performance was disappointing and in reality he faced another couple of races where not much was expected of him until he was allocated a handicap mark.

Only at that point was it possible that he might have become competitive. However, nothing is certain in racing, he had only run once and it was possible that redemption was around the corner. We will never know, H's racing career ended prematurely and he would only be seen again on a point-to-point course. Destined To Shine filled the breach, I was pleased with his efforts and I felt it salvaged the 'partnership' for this reason. After all, with a win and a place in only three runs, he had a 33% strike rate! The horse took me to Warwick, which was a grand day at the races and one of my favourite courses Carlisle, for my exclusive ownership experience. The horse's win at Towcester, was what ownership dreams are made of, and to win under such circumstances and at such prohibitive odds was a quite remarkable achievement. It cannot be stressed enough that to 'own' a horse at the value end of the market and to achieve a winner in such a short space of time, was quite extraordinary. For a lot of 'owners' may never taste a victory, indeed Stan Hey, whose book started this journey, spent a fair amount of money and was never in the winners' enclosure. In my other 'ownership' experiences over the last couple of years I have been lucky enough to have been in the winners enclosure twice before. For DTS to complete the hat trick was the clichéd dream come true.

**The Trainer**
The trainer has a difficult balancing act to perform. On the one hand they want to keep their horse fit, healthy and in training to race, but on the other they want to keep the 'owners' happy with days at the races, and hopefully a win or two. Kerry Lee was in her second season as a trainer and was obviously keen on establishing herself in the ranks of racehorse trainers. A syndicated partnership was surely something she welcomed. The days of the landed gentry providing the training fees have long gone and the self-democratisation of ownership means that syndicated partnerships with such as Foxtrot are much sought after.

She and her father made the 'partners' very welcome at the stable visit days, which were generally pleasant affairs that gave us something of an insight into how the horse was working. Such visits are a key component to the ownership experience; we can meet fellow 'partners', exchange ideas and of course quiz the trainer on all aspects of the horse's progress. Over the year communications with the trainer were adequate and we were informed about key decisions, not least running plans.

Kerry definitely had bad luck with the Indian summer that seemed to scupper any racing for H and clearly there was nothing she could do about his unfortunate injury. I think the Lees did well to provide DTS at such short notice, but it was clearly an arrangement that suited both parties. Richard (who was the man who appeared on all race days) was the old school experienced hand that was passing on the reins, so to speak. It could be that syndicates are a new phenomenon for the old school, but I couldn't have been more impressed with him than I was at Carlisle, where he proved to be a charming and informative man.

The jockeys of course in my opinion are the unsung heroes of this tough sport. Theirs is a demanding job, with a surprisingly low remuneration for putting their body on the line each time they race. When Sam Twiston Davies rode DTS to his moment of glory at Towcester, it was just some months after he had returned from hospital, where he was in an induced coma following a fall at Chepstow. In the context of over paid, over praised sportsman in other fields, I have only the utmost respect for these people and the jobs they perform.

The trainers lot though is a difficult one; they are in a tough business. They have to maintain a string of horses, keep them healthy and fit and provide winners for demanding owners. The number struggling with low strike rates, diminishing horse numbers, limited revenues and in some cases bankruptcy, reflect what a cut throat business it is.

One thing though remains sacrosanct and that is the expert nature of their status, within a syndicate partnership. Kate Fox in her book "the Racing Tribe", labelled the trainer as the witch doctor of the tribe. In that she meant the trainers expertise dictated all the crucial decisions that related to the horse and in that sense they brook no interference. In this 'modern ownership syndicate', this definitely rings true, we must put ourselves in the hands of the trainer, and their decision is final.

**The Syndicate**
Foxtrot proved to be a very impressive syndicate to join. They were, as they said at the outset clear and transparent in all their dealings. This is really important to the ordinary man dipping his toes into the World of racehorse ownership, a World that might appear a shady unreliable place to the uninitiated. You are handing over relatively large sums of money and trust and reliability are paramount.

 Their lines of communication were clear and consistent, and they constantly kept me abreast of developments. By far their greatest achievement was to obtain tickets for 'partners' and guests at all the relevant races. In comparison to my previous 'ownership' experience this was quite a luxury and allowed me to plan for all races, knowing I was guaranteed an owners place on every occasion. At the outset I had given myself the objective of seeing all the horse's races and this of course was achieved. Something that was made a little easier by the fact there were only four races! I had at the planning stage claimed that I would have been satisfied by six race days, so four was a little disappointing.
 However, there were mitigating circumstances that were beyond the control of the syndicate. I know enough to know that there are no guarantees in racing, and that people joining the old 'ownership' game must be prepared to accept whatever racing they get. Foxtrot's efficiency and generous allocation allowed for some excellent race days and in this they achieved the 'owners' number one priority.

## Returns

I had enough previous experience to know that you don't go into horse 'ownership' to make money. As Stan Hey memorably pointed out in his book: 'Owners develop an innate sense of the value they are getting from their involvement with horses, one that doesn't involve prize money'. This is certainly the case; one has to review the overall experience of ownership in its widest sense.

In terms of such 'real owner' experience I believe the project was a success. I did experience the reality of the ups and downs of modern National Hunt racing. Not all the news was good, but it was never less than interesting. Some of the 'partners' were good company with realistic expectations, who were clearly enjoying the overall experience. The stable visits were enjoyable and quite revealing in terms of how a modern stable operates. The beautiful Byton countryside stayed in my minds eye and stimulated further visits.

The horses were safe and sound after one season and as described they brought me to some interesting places. Winning we are told is not so vital, it is the taking part that counts. This in general is true, but there is nothing to compare with your horse actually winning a race. Seeing Sam Twiston Davis pilot DTS around a drenched Towcester and not see another horse in the process was a very special feeling.

For the record, when May arrived Dan faithfully produced a balance sheet for the term, which recorded all expenses and any returns for the season.

In terms of a dividend I received the princely sum of £142, made up of horse winnings and unspent subscriptions. This was approximately a return of about 11% on my initial investment. Obviously there were a limited number of races and although DTS did obtain prize money, it is somewhat lower for bumper races.

More tellingly it's a poor reflection on the dreadful prize money available to both owners and trainers, who are investing money and time for such paltry returns.

Horseracing is a very profitable business. If most owners, trainers and jockeys are not getting much of a financial return, then who is? Well dear reader, I will give you a clue, it's a ten-letter word beginning with B and ending in S!

With the season over I apply my own method of measuring my returns from being part of an 'owners' syndicate. In comparison to other sports I spend a lot of money on, the ownership lark does come with a set of extra benefits that I calculate a value for and then add on to the dividend returns. For each race meeting that I attend, my guest and I gain free entry into what is usually the premier enclosure and as opposed to other sports I attend this is clearly saving me money. Although Towcester was a difficult course to put a value on because of its novel free entry, the access to the owner's section clearly could be evaluated. In addition to this 'owners' are always given complimentary programmes and food and drink. This later aspect can vary enormously from course to course, a hot quality meal at Warwick to tea and biscuits at Towcester. For these extra factors I apply the VAH, (Value Added Horseracing) formula, and this tells me that I gained a further £210! This sum added to the dividend would bring the total to £350, a return of 28% on my original investment, now that reads a lot better!
Finally there is the betting, this I do not include in the VAH. Many people think that as an 'owner' you are privy to all sorts of insider details regarding your horse's prospects.

Over the years, I've never found this to be true. You know when your horse is training well and you can make a realistic assessment of its chances once you see the opposition, but the rest is in the hands of the gods.

Trainers tend to be very nervous regarding their own horses chances and this is not surprising given the amount of time and worry that goes into getting the animal to the races. As the old adage goes, you bet as much as you are prepared to lose. From my perspective, no matter how much of an outsider your horse is, because he is 'your' horse you must always stake a wager on him. It's a mixture of loyalty, blind faith and that in racing nothing is a certainty. AS DTS showed with his heroics at Towcester, you just never know and his actions alone guaranteed a healthy betting return on the horses over the season

With my 'ownership' season at an end, Foxtrot attempted to entice me with further opportunities with some other horses. I was most impressed with them and indeed may return at another time to take up another offer. However, I declined their kind invitations, I had my mind set on other things!

# GLOSSARY

Firstly the horses followed in this book are National Hunt horses. These are Jumps horses racing over obstacles, either fences known as chases or hurdles.

For the uninitiated below are a list of terms used in the book, which you may find helpful.

**BAY –** Deep reddish brown coloured horse

**BHA** – British Horseracing Authority

**Black Type** – a horse that has won or been placed in a pattern/listed race, usually enhances their breeding value.

**Bumper** – national hunt flat race for prospective jumping horses

**Chaser** – a horse, which takes part in, jumps races over fences

**Colours** - The racing silks worn by jockeys, registered by the owner

**Connections** – owners and trainers of a horse.

**Cut in the ground** – the ground surface that has been softened by rain.

**Dam** – the mother of a horse.

**Declared** – a horse is confirmed to start in a race (usually 48 hours in advance for flat horses and 24 hours for jumps).

**Favourite** – the horse on which most money has been wagered

**Frame** – horses finishing in the first three places.

**Furlong** – one eighth of a mile or 220 yards and the distance in which races are measured.

**Gelding** – a male horse that has been castrated.

**Going** – official description of the racing surface, it is determined by the amount of moisture in the ground. This can range from heavy, soft, good and firm.

**Graded races** – the top tier of races. On the flat group 1 is the highest category, with group 2 and 3 in descending order. Over the jumps, the top tier is grade 1 with grade 2 and 3 in descending order.

**Green** – an inexperienced horse

**Handicap** – the BHA allocate a different weight for each horse to carry. After a horse has run usually three times it is allocated an official handicap mark that determines the weight it will carry in a handicap race.

**Hurdler** – a horse that races over hurdles, which are lighter and lower than fences

**Juvenile** – two year old horse

**Length** – the unit of measurement for the winning margin, the measurement of a horse from head to tail

**Listed race** – a class of race just below group (flat) or graded (jumps).

**Maiden** – a horse that hasn't yet won a race.

**Napped** – best bet according to a tipster

**Odds on** – strong favourite, where winnings are less than the stake

**Off the bridle** – a tired horse reduces his effort

**Outsider** – Long priced animal in the betting, viewed as unlikely to win

**Photo Finish** – Electronic photo devise which determines minimal distances in a close finish

**Placepot** – selecting a placed horse in all 6 races at a selected race meeting.

**Pulled up** – a horse that drops out of the race, a non-finisher.

**Rating** – a measure of a horse's ability usually on a scale from 0 to over 100. There are different official rating figures for flat and national hunt horses.

**Ring** – parade ring where connections meet as horse parades.

**Sire** – father of a horse.

**Stallion** – an entire horse used for breeding purposes

**Starting Price (SP)** - Official odds of a horse at which bets are settled

**String** – all the horses in a particular training stable.

**Timber** – racing over hurdles

**Under Starter's Orders** – the time the runners are deemed to be ready to race

**Yearling** – a horse of either sex during 1 January to 31 December following the year of its birth

**End Piece**

In both of my books on racehorse ownership the people I have been most impressed with are the jockeys. Theirs is a challenging profession, constantly risking life and limb and sometimes for very little remuneration. As has been mentioned in both books sometimes there are dreadful accidents that can leave them maimed or even worse.

With this in mind any monies that accrue from the sales of this book and **Four Hooves and a Prayer** *(which can be obtained from amazon.com)* will be directed to the Injured Jockeys Fund (IJF).

Printed in Great Britain
by Amazon